Decoding America

&

Coming Home to Yourself
The Immigrant Experience

SIMONE JOHNSON SMITH

HOST OF THE PODCAST
THE IMMIGRANT EXPERIENCE IN AMERICA

minna PRESS

ISBN Paperback: 979-8-218-54120-0
ISBN eBook: 979-8-3305-0902-7

—Ordering Information—
Special discounts are available for bulk purchases by corporations,
associations, and others. For details, please contact the author at:
info@thebridgeconcepts.org   www.thebridgeconcepts.org

Editor: Lena Joy Rose

Layout and Design: Mark Steven Weinberger

Printed in the United States of America.

Excerpts, with permission, from the *Deep Culture Podcast*, which
explores the psychological impact of intercultural experiences.
To learn more, visit: [Deep Culture Podcast]
https://japanintercultural.org/podcast-2/

—Disclaimer—
This book shares my personal journey, along with contributions from
others, since arriving in the United States. It is a testament to the diverse
and unique experiences of immigrants. While it may resonate with some
readers, it does not represent everyone's experiences nor claim to provide
a definitive account of the immigrant experience. I encourage you to
approach this story with an open mind and kindly ask that you respect
these perspectives, even if they differ from your own.

To Auntie Hyacinth, who pioneered our family's arrival in the United States, thank you for the unknown sacrifices you must have made while so many looked to you.

To my sweet daughter, Saige, may this book serve as a guide, a source of inspiration, and a keepsake of my journey through this shape-shifting world.

CONTENTS

FOR FIVE YEARS, the idea of writing a handbook for immigrants has been nudging at the back of my mind. As immigrants, we often focus on the practicalities of life, chasing after opportunities wherever they lead us. I was no different—I had responsibilities to meet, a house to maintain, and loved ones to support. Though I was single with no children then, the weight of those obligations was ever-present. Still, amidst the hustle and late-night hours, I found myself scribbling down ideas, capturing the inspiration that struck when the world was quiet. Since then, life has evolved in beautiful ways—I got married, welcomed our first child, and continued to grow both personally and professionally. Through it all, the desire to create this handbook has grown stronger each year.

Then, on January 1, 2021, everything changed. My mother, who had bravely battled an illness for over a decade, passed away. The loss hit me hard, much earlier than I had ever imagined facing such a reality. Her passing brought a wave of pain that forced me to rethink my priorities. Burying a parent has a way of sharpening life's focus. It made me realize that if there was something I felt called to do, I could not afford to wait any longer.

That summer, still processing my grief, I joined a mastermind group, and an idea struck me—why not start a podcast? It could be a platform to interview fellow immigrants about their journeys, a space to inspire others while keeping the conversation about our experiences alive. So, I did. By October 2021, the podcast was up and running. Despite resistance from those who were used to seeing me in different roles, I pushed forward. The podcast sparked something within me—joy, passion, and a renewed sense of purpose. It became clear that this was the path I was meant to follow. Something for Simone!

In 2023, I decided this would be my year of saying "No." I hoped that doing so would reclaim my energy and focus on what truly mattered. However, even then, I grappled with immigrant survivor's guilt—a feeling of obligation to support those back home as one of the fortunate few living in a land of perceived abundance. Journaling became a lifeline, helping me gain clarity and reconnect with what was truly important, essentially bringing me back to myself.

EPISODES 85, 86, 87.

I live by example. I make sure to embody the values and lessons I want to impart to my children. For instance, in African and Asian cultures, it is common to look after the people back home when you are abroad. My children know that I do that. I earned this money after working so hard, but it doesn't all come to me. Before I had children, if I made 500 pounds, 300 pounds was sent home. There are children back home where I have to pay their school fees. Some people cannot relate but this is how it is in my culture. When my father died, I went to live with my uncle, who was financially able to help my mother. In our family and community if there are less fortunate people, those more financially better off will usually help. In the UK and in America, some people find that really strange. I try to instill in my children the importance of being there for each other no matter what. I want my children to know my culture, but there are certain parts of it that I do not agree with and that I am forever pushing up against. As much as I don't mind helping families back home, I also know the kind of burden that it is. It can be exhausting, especially if you have done better than the others or you are the eldest. I don't want my children to have that sort of burden, but they are aware of the culture.

As immigrants, many of us come from collectivist cultures where the community's needs often take precedence over individual desires. We are taught to play our part and to carry the burdens of others, sometimes at the expense of our well-being. Yet, the expectation here in the U.S. is that we must assimilate, blend in, and avoid drawing too much attention to ourselves. We are encouraged to change—our accents, clothes, even our physical appearances—to fit into a culture that often seems impossible to please. But where does it stop? When do we stop shapeshifting and start embracing our authentic selves, integrating our cultural heritage with our new environment?

I believe that to survive and thrive in the U.S., we must come home to ourselves and embrace our cultural roots, heritage, accents, and the unique value we bring. So many people chase success and achieve it, only to realize they end up empty.

Through my own journey, I hope to illuminate the challenges faced by immigrants and their children in the United States. These individuals enter the country legally but still struggle to live and thrive despite their sacrifices. They work in jobs that no other American wants to do, for pay that no other American wants, and in conditions under which no other American wants to work. Despite the value they add to American society, they are often stifled.

Packing up and leaving is not always an option. Returning to our previous homes is often impossible due to economic decline, natural disasters, or social unrest. So, we have no choice but to nurture and embrace the places we now consider home.

Simone

Simone Johnson Smith
Author, Life Coach, Speaker, and Podcaster: *The Immigrant Experience in America*

America—The Land of Milk and Honey

THE PHRASE "the land that flows with milk and honey," rooted in the Bible, symbolizes a place of abundance, prosperity, and opportunity—a Promised Land. For many, the U.S. embodies this ideal, a land where dreams can flourish and a better life seems within reach. The allure of this promise drives countless individuals to seek a new beginning for themselves and their families.

In 2022 alone, over 2.8 million people were apprehended and turned away by U.S. Customs and Border Protection. The numbers are staggering: in fiscal year 2023, there were a record-breaking 3.2 million encounters at the border. Yet, despite these barriers, millions more will continue to risk everything in 2024, driven by the hope of partaking in this mythical 'milk and honey.'

The scale of global migration is immense. According to the United Nations International Migration Report, as of 2020, approximately 281 million people were living outside their country of birth—a number that already exceeds some projections for 2050. Since 1970, the global migrant population has tripled, with the U.S. as the primary destination for many. The World Economic Forum highlights that the majority of migrants hail from India, underscoring the U.S.'s enduring appeal as the ultimate land of opportunity.

This relentless pursuit of a better life underscores the powerful allure of the American dream. This dream continues to draw millions despite the challenges and barriers they face along the way.

The allure of immigrating to the United States remains strong, no matter the reason for leaving one's home country. The U.S. continues to attract the largest number of immigrants globally, with 1.5 million people legally migrating in 2021 alone and nearly 2.8 million non-immigrant visas granted in the same year. However, the journey does not end at arrival. Once here, immigrants often face a complex mix of emotions—elation mixed with the challenges of language barriers, culture shock, and economic struggles. As they navigate this new world, they wrestle with holding onto their identity and culture while trying to fit into their new surroundings.

Leaving it All Behind...or Not?

Drawing from personal experience, extensive research, and insights from my podcast interviews, I have concluded that The U.S. can be a place where you might feel pressured to abandon your true self. However, staying true to yourself is the key to surviving and thriving here. It is about finding that delicate balance—assimilating to the new culture while fiercely holding onto your individuality. This balance allows you to integrate the best of both collectivist and individualistic cultural dynamics.

Embracing your immigrant identity in its entirety—including your heritage, accent, skin tone, body shape, and all the unique aspects of who you are—while also understanding and adapting to the norms of your new environment empowers you to stand confidently in your identity. It is not about letting go of your roots; it is about planting them firmly in new soil so you can grow even stronger. In this way, you can positively influence your surroundings, becoming a bridge between two worlds.

In this book, I will explore the importance of embracing your strengths and returning to your authentic self so you can find a true sense of belonging in the immigrant experience. I will also provide practical advice on navigating the complexities of being true to yourself while integrating into your new community and culture.

The Pressure to Conform

Many immigrants across the United States have expressed a concern that deeply resonates with me. When we bring our authentic selves to the U.S. marketplace and daily life, we are often told to assimilate into an elusive, ever-changing concept of "American" culture. Our contributions may have value, but our presence is not always welcomed with open arms. The pressure to conform can be overwhelming, leaving many feeling like they must shed their cultural traditions and values to survive.

This pressure is not just a vague feeling—it has real, lasting consequences. For example, many Spanish-speaking immigrants have historically been discouraged from speaking their native language outside their homes, leading to the loss of oral traditions, history, and language for future generations. This is why immigrants must hold onto their authentic selves and cultural heritage. These aspects of our identity make us unique and valuable, not just to ourselves but to the broader society we are now a part of.

Holding on to who you are is not just an act of resistance but a pathway to thriving. It is about recognizing the immense value of being an immigrant and bringing a wealth of experience, knowledge, and culture that can enrich the American landscape. Moreover, it is about standing tall in the face of adversity, knowing your authenticity is your greatest strength.

Who this Book is For

This book will be a beacon of light or guidepost to:

- First-generation immigrants
- First-generation Americans (children of immigrants)
- Foreign nationals considering migrating to the U.S. and or another Western country
- Everyday Americans and policymakers to educate them about the immigrant experience.

If you are considering moving to the U.S., this book is necessary. It is crucial to think and reflect on the challenges of living in the U.S., especially if you come from certain parts of the world that are deemed unfavorable to the prevailing anti-immigrant sentiments of many.

What You Will Learn from Reading This Book

You will receive insightful recommendations on how to deal with everyday problematic exchanges such as:

1. Dating and marriage in the U.S.
2. Raising a child in a country (the immigrant-mom experience) such as the U.S. with different values, culture, nutrition, and education system from the one in which you were born and raised
3. Navigating the workspaces in the U.S., i.e., being a working mom and having less help in an individualistic society
4. Finding belonging, religion, and the immigrant experience, the struggle deciding whether to assimilate or not to assimilate
5. Navigating boundaries in a collectivist society and becoming American—the struggle
6. Handling faux pas
7. Dealing with racialized interactions and more

In this book, I take you on a journey through my "Coming to America" moments and share the stories of others who have navigated the challenges of living in the United States. With over two decades of experience, I have learned how to successfully navigate the minefields and pitfalls of living in America. I invite you to join me on this collective, introspective journey, where you will discover why it is essential to come home to yourself. By doing so, you, too, can confidently navigate the challenges of living in America and find a sense of belonging.

The New Colossus

Not like the brazen giant of Greek fame,
With conquering limbs astride from land to land;
Here at our sea-washed, sunset gates shall stand
A mighty woman with a torch whose flame
Is the imprisoned lightning, and her name.
Mother of Exiles. From her beacon-hand
Glows worldwide welcome; her mild eyes command
The air-bridged harbor that twin cities frame.
"Keep, ancient lands, your storied pomp!" cries she
With silent lips. "Give me your tired, your poor,
Your huddled masses yearning to breathe free,
The wretched refuse of your teeming shore.
Send these, the homeless, tempest-tost to me,
I lift my lamp beside the golden door!"

CHAPTER 1

All my skinfolk ain't kinfolk.

—Zoria Neale Hurston

My Family's Journey to U.S. Citizenship

Having lived in the U.S. longer than in my birth country, I often find myself asking: Does that make me more American or less Jamaican? It is a question that's crossed my mind countless times, especially when I hear fellow Jamaicans with thick accents suggest that my softened Jamaican accent somehow makes me less Jamaican. These comments usually make me chuckle—it is as if these self-appointed "accent police" believe they hold the authority to decide who is or is not genuinely Jamaican. Yet, I cannot help but notice that these same individuals would proudly claim me as Jamaican if I were to achieve something significant. It is a sentiment echoed by many other immigrant communities—Indians who leave the mainland are often seen as less Indian, and Africans from the continent sometimes view those in the diaspora as "watered-down" versions of themselves.

This struggle with identity is not unique to Jamaicans. Conversations about reconnecting the African continent with its diaspora have become more common in recent years. In 2022, President Biden even signed an executive order to establish the President's Advisory Council on African Diaspora Engagement in the United States to strengthen ties between Africa and its diaspora. While it remains to be seen what this engagement will yield, the conversation itself is telling. Despite whatever definitions may exist about nationality or identity, I know this: My roots run deep in Jamaica. My heritage, my family's land, and our history stretch back at least five generations. Whether Africa or the U.S. fully embraces us, Jamaica will always be home. It is the place where my daughter knows she can return when the U.S. wavers in its welcome towards immigrants.

What is home? The Egyptian writer Naguib Mahfouz once said, "Home is not where you are born; home is where all your attempts to escape cease." If that is the case, my search for home is still ongoing. My family's journey to the U.S. began in August 1998. I vividly remember boarding the Air Jamaica flight and waving goodbye to our family, who had watched it from the waving gallery. We had done this countless times before—waving off other family members as they visited and departed—but it was our turn to leave this time. I had no idea what lay ahead, but we were in for the ride of our lives. Knowing what I know now, would I have left our sweet Jamaica? We have debated that question on our podcast, *The Immigrant Experience in America*, for two years.

I often wondered how our family made it here but never asked until the launch of the podcast in 2022, the passing of our 93-year-old paternal grandma in January 2020, and the transition of our mom on New Year's Day 2021. We jokingly say that Grandma Lou knew the Coronavirus pandemic was coming and wanted to return home. We buried her, returned to the U.S., and the borders closed—the timing was uncanny.

For some reason, something shifted in me. I wanted to know everything about both sides of my family of origin after the passing of Grandma Lou (affectionately known as "*Mah*" to us) and my mother within approximately 11 months. Mom had battled an illness for more than ten years, and it seemed we were never given a reprieve to get to these everyday conversations. Dad and I have spoken more than we have over many years in the U.S. As we planned a celebration of Dad's 70th birthday back on the island, all sorts of conversations started surfacing, and one day in 2023, I asked:

"Dad, how did our aunt get to the U.S.?"

Dad chuckled as he usually does when we surprise him with a question. "She applied to an ad in *The Gleaner*" (one of the major newspapers), he said. "She applied and paid and never heard back from the agency."

"Oh, so that is how it all started?" I exhaled a huge sigh of relief over the phone. I was always nervous to ask due to my work engagements in the immigration space.

"She had to get a lawyer involved to find out what happened. They never replied or found her a job. The lawyer got them to take action on her case, and she moved to the U.S. to work with a family. After your grandpa passed, it was rough for your grandma and us kids," Dad said, as he paused.

After a lengthy pause, Dad continued to explain how my aunt made it to the U.S. "The sponsoring U.S. family filed for her, and she received her green card from this job," he said.

My heart swelled with emotion, and I wiped the tears streaming down my cheeks as we talked. "She started it all," I said. "I wonder what life would've been like for us if we never left Jamaica," I added. "This country has blessed our family so much. I hope the younger generation knows our story and does not get lost here. They need to know this story to appreciate and be more grateful." As I shared my heart, Dad listened.

Dad recounted the story of his oldest sister, Auntie Hyacinth, as she set off on her journey to America, a journey that would alter her family's trajectory for generations. He detailed the drama surrounding her application to an organization that matches people with work opportunities in the U.S. Apparently, the organization took the application and the monies required and never found my aunt a job. They got a lawyer involved, and the organization came clean, which led to my aunt acquiring her green card. Auntie Hyacinth would later sponsor several of her siblings, of which my dad was one (he had waited 12+ years for his visa number to be called). The truth is that I was nervous and apprehensive that there may have been some illegality involved, and I was relieved when I heard that she entered the U.S. legally and received her green card.

Over the years, I had felt like I was hiding in the shadows, like so many immigrants, even though we entered legally, because of messages that I was foreign, spoke with an accent, and should let others win because they were born here. On the one hand, I was a bright-eyed, ambitious young lady who only wanted to excel in academics, as this was where I had a track record of doing well from my formative years in school. I did well in Spanish, French, History, Math, and a few other subjects on the Caribbean Examination Council (CXC) final exams, so I sought to continue my studies.

No one said you had to attend school, but as in many first-generation immigrant families, you know what is expected of you. We are here to take care of business. We work, you all go to school, do well, and maybe take a part-time job to help. I had taken the PSAT/SATs in high school but completely forgot to utilize the avenue of universities that had sent me letters before departing Jamaica. It had been at least a year or two, and I had no idea what had happened to those test papers. As children, we had no idea that immigration papers were being processed. We only found out as the interview at the Embassy came up. So, I applied to a two-year college in Kansas City, Missouri, because that is what some folks around me were doing to get into a 4-year university, which I accomplished soon after.

As with many immigrant families who arrive in the U.S., the family mainly left everything behind, so everyone had to chip in to get us moving financially. My first job was at Kmart! I was so excited. I did everything: sporting goods, jewelry, apparel, layaway, checkout, and customer service wherever they needed me. The manager and I got along well, and I was able to bring on my sister, too. I would take the bus to classes during the day and go to work in the afternoons and weekends. I remember leaving my family on Christmas Day to return to the store to clean up after the Christmas madness of last-minute shopping. Those were some interesting days.

I remember someone asking me whether we had roads or cars in Jamaica, to which I laughed and said we swung from trees. The ignorance (or curiosity) I experienced during my early years was sometimes overwhelming. I remember reminding myself that certain words were spelled differently here, and I tried very hard in classes to learn. I felt so exhausted by it all and not understanding what people meant when they used certain phrases and the search to find people who generically understood me so I could feel a sense of belonging.

I clearly remember returning to the island and feeling the hairs on my skin relaxing with the warmth and welcoming vibe of a sense of home. Still, I could not put language, at the time, to why it was different in the U.S. It would take me years to decode the culture, narrative, behaviors, and workspaces to discover that I was experiencing racism, microaggression, discrimination, and other issues Black, Indigenous, People of Color (BIPOC) people face daily. Learning about racism for the first time was distressing. I was not raised in an environment with such negative sentiments towards people of the African Diaspora. For the first time, I thought, Okay, so this is my skin tone, followed by what does it mean here? I realized I had been raised in a bubble and never faced such conversations or realities.

The older folks did not know much about how to have these types of conversations, so it was definitely not a dinner table conversation. We were one happy bundle as we gathered and opened our homes to many friends, schoolmates, neighbors, and others. Our home in Jamaica was known as one of the big houses in the community, so we had many visitors as we grew up. If there was a funeral, it would be a community gathering; hundreds, if not thousands, came out blocking the streets. That tradition continued; college friends would come home with us and attend holiday dinners. We have a running joke that our family cannot cook in small portions because there were always so many mouths to feed and someone else popping in. Grandma Lou would say, "Let me cook a little extra; one never knows who might stop by." After all, she had practice cooking for 11 children, seven males and four females—all more than 6 feet tall. At her funeral, one close neighbor told the story that he would come by our property to play cricket with my dad and the other brothers, hear the pots knocking together, smell the cooking, and could not wait for Grandma Lou to beckon all the boys that dinner was ready.

Later, I would work and complete my undergraduate degree, learn how to drive, and, thanks to Dad—own my first car, rent my first apartment, go on my first date, and so on. It was exciting yet challenging. The realization that I grew up in a bubble hit me as I left home in the Midwest in 2005 and headed to Washington, D.C., against the backdrop of some asking me why I was leaving the family and others expressing fear of my move to the big city. I loaded a Penske truck, and my dear friend, whom I affectionately call Mr. Herb, and my sister were by my side as we drove from the Midwest to North Bethesda, Maryland. I was so excited to be in the big city but had no idea what would be in store: Times of thrilling excitement exploring D.C., visiting salsa dance spots, trying out the many cuisines (I had no idea I had such curiosity and quite the international palette), meeting new friends and colleagues but so naive and unprepared for the D.C. scene. I had applied to a Foreign Affairs fellowship program (literally on the last day racing to FedEx before they closed the door) after having been denied the Rotary Scholarship twice, the Fullbright Fellowship, and several others.

I had been a bank teller throughout undergrad and started working at State Street Bank right out of undergrad, but I was miserable. I did well in math because I have a type-A personality. I remember asking my teachers what I needed to do to get an A, as nothing less would satisfy me. However, investment banking did not click for me. This was my first major full-time work after Kmart, and I was a teller at a commercial bank part-time while an undergrad. As I recall, the hiring manager at Firstar Bank offered me a job while working in Layaway at Kmart. You never know who is watching or how your interaction with someone will lead to the next opportunity, so move with integrity. I was such an eager worker in my early days, which is why the Kmart manager, Brenda, and I got along so well. I remember the bank manager at Firstar Bank saying to me, "Simone, you never complain. You show up when we need you and do your job." This was me fresh off the boat before seeing the realities of the system at play.

A friend recently reminded me how miserable I was at my first employer after undergrad and how I used to tell him that I could not see myself showing up at that building for 20 years. That is all I could think about. I remember needing more support or help to learn my job, and I struggled. I had always excelled in school, so this was new to me. This unhappiness led to me applying for the fellowship to attend a master's program in D.C. I remember studying for the University entry exams, submitting my application, being invited to D.C. for the interviews, my friend coaching me right before the interviews, and visiting three universities on that short trip. I remember the interview as if it were yesterday at the Holiday Inn in Arlington, Virginia.

As fate would have it, I was selected as one of 20 candidates out of 600+ applicants. I had my colleagues at State Street Bank read the email announcing my selection; I was way too nervous to open it myself. Then I was off, leaving the frigid Midwest and heading to D.C., where I grew up and matured into the woman I am today. For the first time, I realized how privileged I was to arrive in the U.S. legally and go directly to college. I learned of the plight of so many living in the shadows because they had overstayed, entered illegally, or had some other status. For the first time, I realized that not everyone saw me as their friend. I am an open person (friendly but back then still a coconut being away from her safe nest for the first time) by nature and have never been shy to start a conversation with someone new, but I later learned just how segregated America was.

I had always had my family and many cousins and never really needed friends outside the home, though I had them. I was always with our extended family at every event. Well, our dad did not allow us to do anything else anyway. Now I can laugh out loud (LOL) about it. I used to be so frustrated about being so tied down while the boys our age in the family appeared to have more freedom than the girls. When I began feeling like the walls of my apartment were eating me alive, I would take a short trip home for a celebration or holiday, and I returned fully rejuvenated just by being in my family's presence. But that only lasted a month or two, and I would return to feeling empty again. I was around so many people but struggled to trust them. I had seen the faces, the pretense, the facade people would put on. It exhausted me.

This is where I started realizing the impact of racism, the shapeshifting U.S. culture and the search for belonging had on my psyche. I did not have the language to put words to describe what I was feeling, but I knew something was wrong. I no longer felt like myself. I would return home to the island, feel completely different, and then return, and my senses would be on alert again. Who is safe? Who is my group? For the first time, I felt I did not feel welcomed by people who outwardly looked like me but saw me as different. I spoke too properly, 'acted White,' or spoke with an accent. I also felt uncomfortable at Happy Hour, where coworkers would mingle after work at one or more bars for alcoholic drink specials and free *hors d'oeuvres*. Back home, we were not raised to barhop but to have dinners at home with friends, and now I had to learn how to decode this scene. Looking back now, I realize I was suffering from anxiety. During the entire 10-year period I lived in the D.C. area, I constantly felt like an imposter and searched for belonging. It felt like I had no one. Shout-out to the West Indian hiking group, Dr. Bobbi and Cheryl March, who took my cousin and me under their wings on hiking and other Caribbean events around D.C. and the Immanuel's Church (no longer exists) for being my family away from home. The people who knew me were miles away, and after being away, living overseas for two years at a time, and in and out of the country for the majority of over ten years, it started to feel like the bonds I once had were withering away. I had been on a plane more than I cared to count and missed many everyday happenings. I did not blame them. I was only one person and could not keep up with everyone. My attempts to call everyone and announce my arrival or departure became exhausting, and many took it way too personally when I could not call or visit in person.

At work, the slights and side comments, which I now know were microaggressions, had worn me down, and I suffered burnout. It can be exhausting being a more melanated-immigrant person. There was no support for decoding the structures and the shapeshifting culture, and I did not know who to trust (as it could be used against you) because the people who looked like me did not see me as a part of their posse. I had an out-of-body experience for several years.

Not being able to share myself authentically worked against me because I was not connecting, and I could not find the words to explain to those around me. Being afraid to share myself and not knowing how much or how little to share was tiring. Often, people see us as golden children who are successful but cannot truly see our humanity. As immigrant children, we have to keep pushing through the clouds, the emotions, the loss of one's cultural self, and the search for belonging (not being accepted by those who do not look like you or the ones who look like you is painful) being seen as a threat to people's jobs and roles, and more but we have to keep walking on water because of the community and cultural expectations. That naive, bright-eyed immigrant girl had to wake up to the new world she was now living in. I was no longer on a small farm where everyone embraced and smiled with warmth and looked out for me. I had no idea that all my value could be boiled down to a straightforward identifier—what shade/tone my skin was and how I physically appeared. It was a hard pill to swallow. If I were to survive and teach my daughter how to survive and thrive here, I had to wake up to the reality of my new country and come home to myself.

PRESSURE TO SUCCEED AND OVER-RESPONSIBILITY
OF FIRST GEN-IMMIGRANT CHILDREN

I would say that the hardest part about growing up as a child of immigrants is that the cultural beliefs in the household are so different than living in America. Like you're taught in our house, don't speak up. Don't rock the boat. Don't do all those things. And then, in the outside world, what is appreciated is you speaking up. In class, you've got to raise your hand, and you've got to speak up in corporate America, you've got to speak up. And that piece was tough. The other tough piece was when my parents would come to get me [after school]. Other kids would make fun of their accents. And they would say, ching-chang-chong. That was hard for me. So, I was embarrassed about my parents, and I just wished I could have parents who could speak "normally." I think the other piece is about being made fun of at school. As a kid, my name was made fun of; my parents were made fun of, and my lunches were made fun of. My parents would pack my favorite thing—mapo tofu. It's a Chinese dish, but it looks mushy. And it's brown, so it's not the most visually appealing, and other kids would make fun of me and say, "Oh, are you eating barf? I'm like, okay, I want to eat peanut butter jelly sandwiches from now on. So, it's that desire as a child to want to fit in with everyone else.

My mom's first job was working at a hotel in Arlington, Virginia, and she commuted an hour and a half each way [on] public transportation to do housekeeping... But my parents didn't speak English. So, they were limited in their opportunities. And so, when they came, they had to learn English. Their income was barely making it because they also had to send money back to my grandparents because my grandparents were taking care of my sisters. My dad always tells me that there was just so much pressure...so much pressure to save all this money, but then you're limited because you've got this three-year contract. And then you've got a two-year-old back in Hong Kong, whose life is depending on you. Being able to establish your roots here fast is essential.

Have you been so busy always catching every ball and fixing, helping, and rescuing, so much so that you have entirely neglected who you are? I have come to realize that codependency is common in collectivist cultures, which are also high on interdependence and community cohesion. Since 2013, I have been on a journey of finding my voice, myself, joy, and peace. Since then, I have unearthed feelings that I never knew lay dormant within the crevices of my soul.

I recently interviewed Amy Yip, A Somatic Life Coach and author of *Unfinished Business: Breaking Down the Great Wall Between Adult Child and Immigrant Parent.* I have conducted over 100 interviews with immigrants discussing their journeys of adaptation, growth, and struggle, but none hit me quite like her story. The tears started pouring, and I could not maintain my composure for the rest of the interview. Suddenly, visions of how I had neglected myself flooded my world without end.

I looked around and recognized the patterns of constant rescue and heartbreak. I finally recognized that over the years, the people I had rescued could not help me. I had been so busy doing, fixing, and rescuing that I could not see what was happening around me. For example, the people who would come into my life to fill their cups or were with me only because they enjoyed the light shining from my essence. If you are a first-generation immigrant challenged by the constant hyper-achievement, doing some research into generational trauma, childhood or other traumas in your life may help uncover what is driving you to resort to this behavior. You may need the support of a life coach and a community of people having similar challenges to help you navigate such a journey.

Look around you. Who is in your inner circle? Who is around? Are they there for you? Are they able to pour back into you as you fill their cup? Are they good for you? Over-responsibility, hyper-achievement, and codependency appear to have ruled me without my full knowledge and awareness. In 2023, I decided to stop. To stop the doing, the chasing, the traveling, the fixing, the rescuing, the saving, the sending of financial support, the calling, everything. This was my year of "No."

I needed to see who and what remained when I said no, when I stopped talking, stopped doing, stopped rescuing, stopped saving. What would remain after I stopped scurrying about so my emotions could settle, so the fatigue and unending anxiety to please could subside? It was here that I saw that I was on an island all by myself. The phone stopped ringing. Then, I noticed I was still attracting people who thought I could do something for them, even via my podcast and social media interactions. If I do not learn this lesson by coming home to myself and going within to observe the

REALIZING HOW SEGREGATED AMERICA
AND THE CHURCH ARE

This is the American culture, and I did not realize that there are many different aspects to the American culture. When I came to the U.S., I was part of the African American culture; that was absolutely my first time learning... Black history and learning about segregation and racism and all the things I didn't have an Intellectual understanding of coming from Trinidad. In the beginning, I remember us international students being very judgmental about the African American students, almost like, why can't they get their act together? I think it took several years before I realized or understood the nuances of that culture and even came to appreciate it. Then, I went to the other side, and my experience was different. I wasn't invited to share about myself or asked about my culture... And I started to see, 'Oh, my goodness,' it's a whole different world out here. And I think that's when I became more aware of the race dynamic because I saw it. I was feeling it.

My primary struggle with America is understanding race relations and how it impacts our relationships. And not finding deep, intimate connections outside the Black community. As immigrants, we tend to be more open-minded and inclusive; we can be friends with anybody red or yellow, Black, or White. Right. We will be friends with White people, all the people. And then you start to realize that they may not want to be friends with you. And I didn't know how I did not know that until like ten years later. My breaking point was the 2016 general election. I felt bad that people were willing to overlook racism, bigotry, and xenophobia which means... My family is overlooked. My husband is overlooked. My Black child is overlooked; for me I felt it deep in my heart because it was mainly tied to the church. And the whole White and Black differences in the church. I knew it was real. And I think the reality of it is real at my core.

patterns and cycles in my life, I will be here again in one year, five years, or ten years. As scary as it felt, I had to face the shadows following me around.

The immigrant mentality is interesting in this culture, and one must be careful not to get lost. Many immigrants from collectivist cultures tend to be responsible and are action-oriented problem solvers. In the collectivist setting, this dynamic works well. You give, and everyone gives, and your cup gets filled; well, most times. In the individualistic culture, what is in it for me is that people take and leave. As a first-generation immigrant, your light often shines so bright in serving others and always rescuing that you often do not realize you attract dependent personalities with nothing to pour back into you. They have been feeding off your energy and light. When you stop playing the role or shed that part of your personality that no longer serves you, those dependent personalities will disappear as sure as daybreak.

CHAPTER 2

*America is the Place Where
You Come to Lose Yourself and Find Yourself.*

Becoming American

We have been here before—America's wrestle with whether immigration is a medicine it wants to take. The fear of immigration runs deep. It has been part of the American narrative since the country's inception. Why does it feel like most of the U.S. is anti-immigration? If one listens to the daily news bytes, all immigrants (both legal and illegal) need to hasten back to their lands of origin as we are not welcomed in the United States. These sentiments can be especially loud towards people from the African Diaspora.

I recently had a well-informed friend explain the impact of the Civil Rights movement and the Civil Rights Act on immigration. It helped me understand some of my experiences as an Afro-Caribbean person in this country. Many immigrants entering the United States are oblivious to many of the political and other backdrops at play. For instance, I was particularly intrigued by the ousting of news anchor, Don Lemon from CNN after a heated conversation with an Indian political candidate regarding the Civil Rights Act's influence on the Immigration and Nationality Act (INA). This left me questioning what Mr. Lemon meant and why it felt so personal for him. Media reports suggest that Mr. Lemon was let go due to allegations of mistreatment of colleagues. However, others cite his interview with the political candidate (obviously of an immigrant heritage), schooling him about his experience as a black native-born male in the United States. Mr. Lemon went on to explain that the Civil Rights Act opened the door for immigrants as the reason. Since I had not studied this part of American history, I began the research to understand it better. According to the U.S. Conference of Catholic Bishops, "On January 8, 1964, President Lyndon Johnson delivered his State of the Union Address. Here, he called for the abolition of all forms of racial discrimination—calls that anticipated the passage of the Civil Rights Act some six months later—and committed his Administration to 'lifting by legislation the bars of discrimination against those who seek entry into our country.'"

Prior to the 60s, most immigrants to the U.S. hailed from Europe and Canada. The Pew Research Center reports that in 1960, 84 percent of immigrants in the U.S. originated from these regions, with a mere 6 percent from Mexico, 3.8 percent from South and East Asia, 3.5 percent from Latin America, and 2.7 percent from other regions worldwide. Fast forward to 2017, and the landscape has shifted dramatically. European and Canadian immigrants constituted just 13.2 percent, while those from Mexico comprised 25.3 percent, other Latin American countries 25.1 percent, Asia 27.4 percent, and other regions nine percent.

The history of immigration in the United States reflects a rich tapestry of diverse cultures and stories. Each wave of immigrants has contributed to the nation's identity, bringing unique challenges and enriching the American experience. The shifts in immigration patterns mirror what is happening on a global level as well as the changing policies within the U.S. The iconic words inscribed on the Statue of Liberty symbolize America's long-standing image as a beacon of hope for those searching for freedom and opportunity. Nevertheless, the reality has been complex, with the nation's welcome mat being extended and retracted in response to various economic, political, and social pressures.

As described, the shift in demographics, alongside a deeper comprehension of the Civil Rights Act and the Immigration and Nationality Act, has shed light on my personal journey as an immigrant. An Op-Ed by Robert Cherry further enlightened me that affirmative action appears to benefit Blacks but not native-born Blacks in the United States.[ii]   I have often pondered the reason behind the palpable animosity I sometimes encounter from native-born African Americans. Now, I have gained insight into the historical context that shapes current attitudes, allowing me not to take any perceived hostility personally, though it is challenging to maneuver and manage. As the famous reggae singer Jimmy Cliff sings, *I can see clearly now that the rain is gone. All of the bad feelings have disappeared.*

The conversation around the dynamics between native-born African Americans and those of African descent from other regions is profound. Harvard Professors Henry Louis Gates, Jr., and Lani Guinier pointed out that a considerable number of Black students at Harvard are either immigrants themselves or the children of immigrants from West Indian and Continental African backgrounds. This contrasts with native-born African Americans whose lineage in the United States extends back generations and who have been directly impacted by slavery, Jim Crow, and other systems.[iii] Professors Guinier and Gates, Jr. highlight that the quota set to address historical and systematic barriers to African American entry to Ivy League institutions was missing the intended outcome. Armed with this knowledge, I can empathize and have more informed conversations about race, identity, and the legacy of historical policies on our current populations.

The idea that immigrants, especially from the African diaspora, should have a foundational understanding of U.S. history before moving here is a salient one. It suggests that such knowledge could significantly impact one's assimilation and interpretation of social norms. With this historical context, we are better equipped to discern the nuances of this daily American life.

Understanding this nuanced history is crucial for comprehending the current state of immigration and the experiences of those who come to the United States seeking a new beginning. It is a narrative that continues to unfold, shaping the country's future and its ongoing dialogue about identity, belonging, and the meaning of being "American." While living in the D.C. metro area, I had a firsthand experience of a White male telling me that he was afraid of immigrants taking what he had. The fear is real. The typical hustle and industrious mentality of newly arrived immigrants was my reality. Everything I have accomplished since moving to the U.S. was not without sacrificing luxury, leisure, and delaying gratification. I knew no immigrant who had wrongfully taken anything such as land, employment, or anything else from a native-born person, though this may be debatable. However, the historical narrative was packed with stories contrary to others doing just that to other groups.

The Case for Immigration and its Positive Impact on the U.S.

The sentiment that immigrants are taking jobs and resources is a common concern in immigration discussions. However, the U.S. economy has historically been a capitalist system that thrives on a continuous supply of inexpensive labor. This demand has been met in various ways throughout history, from the abhorrent practice of slavery to the use of indentured servants and, more recently, through the legal immigration of both skilled and unskilled workers to address labor shortages.

1. Could the U.S. Survive Without Immigrants?

This question is satirically explored in the mockumentary "A Day Without a Mexican," in which all Mexicans suddenly disappear from California. The film serves as a social commentary, humorously highlighting the crucial roles that Mexican immigrants play in the state's daily life and economy. The film raises thought-provoking questions about the often-underappreciated work performed by this community, from domestic chores to maintenance, agriculture, and food service industries.

In essence, the film delves into a hypothetical society without immigrants:

- Who would clean the toilets?
- Who would fix the roofs?
- Who would do the landscaping?
- Who would pick the plants and pick the tomatoes?
- Who would be working in the back of restaurants?
- Who would fill the IT jobs and the hard sciences?
- Who would work on rural chicken farms doing the work other Americans do not want to do?

Reflecting on the questions posed by "A Day Without a Mexican" brings to light the indispensable role immigrants play in the U.S. economy. The film underscores that we are not here seeking handouts but are integral to the functioning of the capitalist system. With a lucid understanding of the challenges of illegal immigration, I challenge policymakers and society to shift the narrative from criticism to a deeper appreciation for this diverse workforce. Recognizing the value of every worker's contribution, regardless of origin, is essential in maintaining the nation's prosperity and cultural richness.

2. Making the Case for Immigrants

Immigration into the U.S. has been influenced by push and pull factors. Some push factors include political persecution, environmental natural disasters (drought, famine), social unrest (wars, gang violence), economic poverty, low economic activity, and poor job prospects in immigrants' home countries. Among the pull factors are education aspirations, job opportunities, and family reunification. The issues behind push migration run deep. In this global economy, trade gains in country A often result in losses in other places; for example, in the case of the North American Trade Agreement (NAFTA), Mexico, Jamaica, and the dairy industry are among the case studies. Aside from the use of slavery, indentured labor, and other forced forms of labor, immigrants are needed and are essential for the survival of the U.S. economy.

In modern times, with laws prohibiting all forms of forced labor (though it still exists on the books in some states regarding incarcerated individuals), immigration is essential to fueling the U.S. labor engine. It can be argued that the U.S. cannot survive without immigrant labor, cheap labor, and immigration. Americans like their comforts and will not put in the same efforts that immigrants do to keep this economic machine going.

Here are some major points to reflect on regarding the profound impact of immigration:

- According to a Forbes report, **"Immigrants boost economic growth, employment growth, and economic dynamism** through their contributions to the workforce, entrepreneurial activities, and purchases of goods and services."

- In another study, the Foundation for American Policy finds **"that immigrants may slow the offshoring of manufacturing activity by U.S. businesses,** indicating the importance of immigration to increasing U.S. domestic manufacturing production."

- Another Forbes report says, "We find **immigrants represent 16% of all U.S. inventors, but produced 23% of total innovation output,** as measured by number of patents, patent citations, and the economic value of these patents,"[v] according to a National Bureau of Economic Research (NBER).[vi] The American Immigration Council reports, **"44.8% of Fortune 500 companies in 2023, equating to 224 companies, were founded by immigrants or their children."** Further, "These New American Fortune 500 companies collectively generated a staggering $8.1 trillion in revenue during fiscal year 2022, surpassing the Gross Domestic Product (GDP) of several developed nations. Their significant contributions extend beyond revenue, as **they employ over 14.8 million people, emphasizing their role as a crucial driver of job creation and economic prosperity."**

- According to a new National Foundation for American Policy (NFAP) analysis, **"Immigrants have founded or cofounded nearly two-thirds (65% or 28 of 43) of the top AI companies** in the United States."[viii]

- According to the Kauffmann Foundation,[ix] which tracks immigrant entrepreneur trends:

  28% of Main Street business owners are immigrants, even though immigrants comprise just 16% of the labor force and 18% of overall business ownership.

  53% of grocery stores, 45% of nail salons, 43% of liquor stores, 38% of restaurants, and 32% of clothing and jewelry stores are immigrant-owned.

  48% of overall growth of business ownership in the U.S. between 2000 and 2013 was attributed to immigrant business owners.

- A 2012 White House report[x] indicates that immigrants help build and strengthen our economy.

- An article from Forbes posits that reducing immigration harms the American economy. The article also states that immigrants are 30 percent more likely to start a business in the U.S. than non-immigrants, forming 18 percent of all U.S. small business owners. Immigrants added $2 trillion to the U.S. GDP in 2016 and about $460 billion to state, local, and federal taxes in 2018.[xi]

The Deep-Rooted Fear of Immigration

The historical fear of immigration, known as xenophobia, runs deep. It has been part of the American narrative since the country's inception. The history of anti-immigrant sentiment in the United States is a complex and often troubling aspect of the nation's past. Here are some key points that highlight this history:

- The Alien and Sedition Acts of 1798: "These were some of the earliest laws that reflected anti-immigrant sentiment. The acts extended the residency requirement for American citizenship and allowed for the deportation of immigrants deemed dangerous or from enemy nations during wartime."[xii]

- 19th Century: "The rapid increase in immigration, especially from Eastern European countries heightened anti-immigrant feelings. This period saw the rise of nativist groups who opposed immigration on economic, cultural, and racial grounds."[xiii]

- Chinese Exclusion Act: "In 1882, this act was passed to prevent all immigration of Chinese laborers, reflecting the racial prejudice of the time."[xiv]

- Early 20th Century: "Anti-immigrant sentiment continued to grow, leading to the Immigration Act of 1924, which established quotas that severely limited immigration from certain countries."[xv]

- Contemporary Times: "In recent years, anti-immigrant sentiment has often been intertwined with issues of national security, economic competition, and cultural identity. This has led to various policies and debates over immigration reform."[xvi]

The topic of immigration is indeed complex and multifaceted. Anti-immigrant sentiments have been influenced by a wide range of factors, including, but not limited to, economic fears, cultural differences, and national security concerns. This shows how past patterns influence today's political discourse. Despite these seemingly insurmountable challenges, the United States has also seen strong pro-immigrant advocacy groups and individuals working to create a more inclusive society.

The immigrant population who remains and attempts to integrate and assimilate into their adopted country can face many struggles on the journey to 'becoming' part of the local culture. These struggles include, but are not limited to: loss of cultural identity, culture shock, work-life balance, accent bias, search for belonging, and raising children in a culture that is different from the one they were raised in. In addition, there are many challenges that come along with the differences in cultural mindsets about parenting, among other challenges. According to Globalcitizen.org, the top seven challenges facing refugees and immigrants are as follows:

1. Difficulty learning and speaking English

2. Raising children and helping them succeed in school

3. Securing work

4. Securing housing

5. Accessing services

6. Transportation

7. Cultural barriers.

The site references an incident reflecting the impact of cultural barriers to understanding each other:

In Utah, a group of Latter-Day Saints were organizing a week-long hike for youth in the desert. Some organizers thought it might be a nice idea to include some of the refugee youth to integrate them into the community and help them make friends with some of the local kids. "I remember hearing about this and thinking it was such a wonderful idea." ("Seven of the Biggest Challenges Immigrants and Refugees Face in the U.S."). But, less than a day into the hike, some of the refugee kids became very upset. The hike, it turned out, reminded them of when they were forced to flee their homes. Despite the group's kindest intentions, these kids were being retraumatized. This shows how easy it is for these cultural misunderstandings to occur."[xvii]

This incident serves as a powerful reminder of the importance of cultural sensitivity and understanding. It emphasizes the need to consider individuals' unique backgrounds and experiences, especially when organizing events or activities involving participants from diverse cultural backgrounds. By reflecting on this example, we can strive to create more inclusive and respectful environments that honor and consider the perspectives of everyone involved.

Ethnocentrism in America

Ethnocentrism significantly impacts an immigrant's social interactions and can lead to misunderstandings and conflicts. According to Merriam-Webster, ethnocentrism is the attitude that one's own group, ethnicity, or nationality is superior to others. Ethnocentrism is at play in every corner of the United States and many other multicultural spaces around the world. Why does ethnocentrism occur? According to the *Deep Culture Podcast*:

> "…ethnocentrism often feels good. It gives a sense of security and solidarity in a hostile world filled with others. Ethnocentrism can become a breeding ground for prejudice. Can ethnocentrism be overcome by education, or is it natural? To go beyond ethnocentrism, there needs to be a fundamental shift of the acceptance of the legitimacy of other cultures. Go beyond our tendency to split the world into us and others." (Episode 30).

From my insights and observances gained as an immigrant, and in discussion with many immigrants, ethnocentrism can manifest in the United States in the following ways:

1. **Cultural Practices:** Many people carry a cultural pride about their homeland that often shows up as ethnocentrism. 'This is how we do it back home,' some say. Others debate who cooks better or other cultural norms. Some will engage in verbal fistfights with others over why their way of thinking, doing things, or behaving is superior to others. This can be friendly competition or can become hostile among friends and frenemies. One practice that exists with immigrants is that they tend to socialize exclusively with each other, creating enclaves that limit interaction with other groups and the influence of wider local culture. Remaining in an enclave can often work against an immigrant's progress in developing language and cultural competence in their new home. This is why one can experience someone living in the U.S. for 20, 30, or more years and not being able to speak English. Another example of ethnocentrism is when some immigrants view typical leisure activities or child-rearing practices of other cultures as silly, primitive, or inferior. Be mindful of ethnocentric tendencies and suspend ethnocentric evaluations. By that, I mean comparing your home culture with the new culture. Comments like "This is not how we do things back home" and "We do things better back home" may not help you transition and get to the healthy balance of the collectivist and individualistic cultural dynamic you seek.

2. **Language Expectations:** In America, it is expected that everyone should speak English. Immigrants are especially resented when they have lived in this country for 20+ years and do not know a word of English. Preferring to use one's native language exclusively can hinder communication and reinforce the very divisions that we, as immigrants, try to break down. In places known for their linguistic diversity, such as Montreal or Quebec, there is an expectation that these French-speaking people should communicate in English.

3. **Food Judgments**: Of all the cultural baggage we carry from our home country, none is more prominent than our food practices. The types of food we eat and enjoy may be viewed as distasteful, weird, or even revolting to Americans. For example, curry goat or ackee from Jamaica, guinea pigs from Peru, frog legs from France, kangaroos from Australia, and chicken feet from the African Diaspora.

4. **Industrial/Technological Judgments**: The perception that immigrants from less developed regions are backward or inferior is a stereotype that has been challenged and debunked by numerous studies and historical evidence. Immigrants from all parts of the world have contributed significantly to the development of this country, bringing diverse skills, knowledge, and cultural richness.

5. **Economic Tensions:** In many regions of America, there can be a perception that certain immigrant groups are taking over particular industries or job markets, popularly known as 'cornering the market,' leading to tensions between different ethnic communities. For example, Mexicans in landscaping, or Italians in construction. These tensions escalate when these immigrant groups only hire workers from their own ethnic backgrounds.

American Exceptionalism, *Bing!*

Sitting in an eclectic Airbnb in Rossville, GA, at the crack of dawn on a spring day, a visceral *"bing"* went off in my head, body, and spirit. Finally, I understand some of the behaviors one would classify as American. The idea of American Exceptionalism[1] underlies it all. I remember one experience as if it were yesterday when I conversed with a White male in the D.C., Maryland, Virginia (DMV) area

---

1 American Exceptionalism— the belief that the United States is either distinctive, unique, or exemplary compared to other nations

around the holidays at work as each office team tried to decorate a door in something representing Christmas. I wanted to do something personifying my favorite Christmas movie, "Home Alone," the original, not the parts 2, 3, or any following versions. Grandma Lou brought it back on one of her many visits to the U.S. while we were growing up. I remember us gathering around the one TV; everyone spread out in the many corners of the living room, veranda, and mountain-high step in front of the house to watch. Overseas, this became my Christmas tradition, the only movie I must watch, and I belly laugh every Christmas as if I were seeing it for the first time. The influence of American media at its best. So, back to the office story. This young man asked whether I knew "A Christmas Story," I had not. The look on his face said everything. I had had many conversations with other native-born Americans in the past, and the one prevailing message was how ignorant they all were about the rest of the world. I left the conversation viscerally feeling in my body and thinking to myself, the audacity of this male to think that though I was born and raised in another country, I should know everything about American culture. However, he knew little or nothing about my birth country and potentially about many other places around the world. As I sat in the living room of the Airbnb in the Deep South, reading about the origins, history, and progression of the term American Exceptionalism, suddenly, it all made sense. *"Bing!"*

The following references the idea of American Exceptionalism in greater detail:

(a) Exceptionalism seems like a perfectly unexceptional concept—until one asks what it means. Users of the term will then offer specific, but often conflicting, definitions or greet the question with a bewildered stare.

Exceptionalism is evidently a far less obvious idea than most suppose. Instead, different views have been influenced by different sources, including (besides religion) various philosophical doctrines, applications of scientific theories, and reasoning based on political-historical analysis. The exaggerated emphasis on religion may have begun as an innocent error of scholarly interpretation. However, it is being perpetuated today by those seeking, for political purposes, to discredit any possible idea of a political mission in the conduct of foreign affairs.

Until recently—say the last two or three years—few outside the academic world ever encountered the term "exceptionalism." It was reserved almost exclusively for scholarly discourse, used mostly by social scientists and occasionally by historians and students of American studies. Today, "exceptionalism" is used widely in political speeches, newspaper columns, and blog posts. It is often used to divide liberals and conservatives, with liberals generally criticizing exceptionalism, either openly or more subtly to avoid backlash. Liberals would like Americans to think of America as being more "ordinary" and in step with the advanced democracies in the world. In domestic politics, "ordinary" means an expanded welfare state, policies that promote greater income equality, and— it goes without saying—a network of high-speed trains. In foreign affairs, it refers to an America that does not always tout itself as the main world power, is more solicitous of the international community, and does not proclaim a universal standard of right deriving from the "laws of nature."

Although liberals may not say so directly, they want to take America down a notch—and this very sincerely for its own good. Liberals are anti-exceptionalists, deploring the spiritedness and narrow form of patriotism they see as connected with the concept. Like Stephen Walt of Harvard University, they like to proclaim "the myth of American Exceptionalism," pointing out that the doctrine makes it "harder for Americans to understand why others are…often alarmed by U.S. policies and frequently irritated by what they see as U.S. hypocrisy." U.S. foreign policy would be "more effective if Americans were less convinced of their own unique virtues and less eager to proclaim them" (Walt 2011). Conservatives have rallied around exceptionalism, often passionately. Conservatives want Americans to think of themselves as special, and they take great pride in pointing out how America is unlike other advanced democracies. In domestic affairs, conservatives prefer a more limited government, which they consider the cornerstone of liberty; they favor an economy in which incomes reflect market forces, not government decisions; and they, of course, champion travel by stagecoach. In foreign affairs, conservatives hold the idea of the nation in high esteem and bristle at the notion of America being governed by diktats of the international community. They regard America as the premier world power and, therefore, necessarily and rightly subject to different rules than other nations.

Conservatives are not embarrassed to refer to general concepts of right in the terms used by past American statesmen."[xviii] Despite the phrase's relative recency, the idea of Americans as a specially blessed people can be traced back to the Puritan colonists of 17th-century New England, who thought God had chosen them to lead the world by example. Puritan leader John Winthrop illustrated this idea in 1630 by likening the Puritan colony of Massachusetts Bay to a "City upon a Hill," a metaphor still popular among proponents of American Exceptionalism. A sense of divine purpose has remained an important component of American identity for many Americans since then. (Encyclopedia Britannica).

In the 1840s, for example, Jacksonian Democrats (see Andrew Jackson) advocated for annexing the American West by speaking of the United States Manifest Destiny—a God-given mission to extend the American people's way of life across the continent. The same reasoning would be used again in the 1890s to rationalize expansion outside North America and, in the 20th century, to oppose communist governments worldwide. Critics of the notion of American Exceptionalism argue that belief in the concept is unwarranted and seek to reveal the fallacy of the idea of the United States as a virtuous nation by citing examples of its wrongdoing. For example, they respond to the idea that the United States has always been concerned with human rights by raising the country's history of slavery and the expulsion of Native Americans from their land. Believers in American Exceptionalism usually counter such examples of American immorality by casting them as instances of the country falling short of its ideals.

Because believers in American Exceptionalism have skewed Republican in the 21st century, this way of life usually includes a reverence for the Judeo-Christian God, advocacy of a free market, and the prioritization of individual rights over the needs of the collective. Skeptics also compare the concept of American Exceptionalism to the now-discredited views of previous world powers' citizens. Many subjects of the British Empire, it is noted, once thought that they carried "the White man's burden" of civilizing other peoples. French and Portuguese colonists once believed themselves on a "civilizing mission." More recently, the Soviet Union rationalized its own imperialism as a Marxist-Leninist mission of liberation. Proponents of American Exceptionalism reject these parallels as being apples-to-oranges comparisons.[xix]

(b) To a considerable degree, the essence of American Exceptionalism–a nation-state with a special mission to bring freedom to all mankind–depends on the "otherness" of the outside world, so often expressed in the Manichean categories of New World versus Old or free world vs. slave. However, at the heart of the idea lies an odd contradiction. American freedom is generally held to derive from a specific national history and unique historical circumstances–the frontier, the qualities of the Anglo-Saxon race, a divinely appointed mission, and so forth–yet Americans claim universal relevance for their experience and ideals. At its best, the idea of American Exceptionalism carries with it healthy pride in the freedoms Americans enjoy. However, the insistent claim for exceptionalism goes along with national hubris and closed-mindedness and offers an excuse for ignorance about the rest of the world. Since the United States is so exceptional, there is no point in learning about other societies, as their histories have no bearing on ours.

(ethicsandinternationalaffairs.org)

The Immigrant Alchemy Process: Assimilation, Accommodation, Integration—The Immigrant Experience and Finding Belonging

Immigrants are not stats and figures in a report. If you have ever emigrated, you know that feeling deep on the inside of not quite fitting in. Are you still searching for home and the deep sense of belonging you once felt in your birth country? You've studied your adopted country, and you take cues from other immigrants and native-born people about how to navigate or assimilate, but you still feel like a foreigner, alien even to this new world. These are my sentiments exactly for the past two decades as I attempt to understand my life in the United States. Constantly striving but never actually fitting in or feeling accepted, leaving me with a constant yearning for "home."

For many immigrants, finding belonging outside of their birth country can be a painful, disorienting, and deeply personal undertaking. Many find themselves in *the between*, known as a third culture, feeling like a foreigner in both one's birth and adopted countries.

What is culture?

According to Edward T. Hall, "Culture hides more than it reveals, and strangely enough, what it hides, it hides most effectively from its own participants."

Culture is learned. Culture teaches us how to think, conditions us how to feel, and instructs us how to act, especially how to interact with others—in other words, how to communicate. Australian anthropologist Roger Keesing argues that culture provides people with an implicit theory about how to behave and how to interpret the behavior of others.

What shapes culture?

Collectivism and individualism are key components in shaping culture.

As recently as the end of the 20th century, most of the world, about 70%, was collectivist (Triandis 1995). Collectivist cultures tend to be known for traits such as:

- Group harmony and unity
- Family and community focus. An example of blurred lines in parenting occurs when multiple individuals are involved in raising a child
- Modesty and humility.

On the other hand, individualistic cultures have traits such as:

- Personal autonomy and independence – you have noted this if you're in a Western country
- Nuclear family emphasis
- Self-promotion.

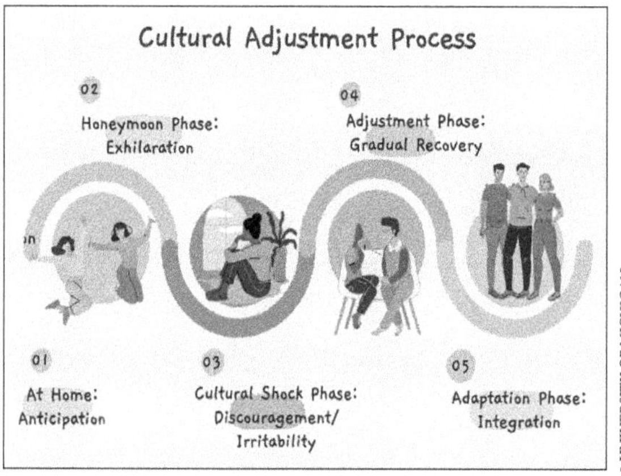

It is important to note that no culture is purely collectivist or individualistic, and elements of both orientations can vary in any society. Additionally, cultural orientations may evolve and change over time due to globalization, migration, and other societal influences.

Most of us are from collectivist cultures, and this has tremendous value. Most developing countries tend to be collectivist, as there is value in sharing limited resources and cooperation. While collectivist cultures have many valuable traits, some can be misused and abused. Immigrants must remain true to their roots as a foundation for a healthy adjustment in an adopted country. Adopted countries can be places where immigrants come to forget who they are. Remember—when you leave home, do not forget who you are!

Let us ponder something that many of us can easily relate to. According to the

Oxford Dictionary, culture shock is "the disorientation experienced by someone suddenly subjected to an unfamiliar culture, way of life, or set of attitudes." Culture shock usually happens at the intersection of clashing collectivist and individualistic values. Coming from a collectivist culture is an important part of our identity for many of us.

Let us look at why culture shock impacts immigrants so profoundly.

Researchers Gullahorn and Gullahorn introduced the W curve model in 1963 to explain the effect of adaptation on immigrants and university students.

As you see in the illustration—the 'W' curve represents the fluctuations of emotions travelers or, in our case, migrants experience when adapting to a new culture.

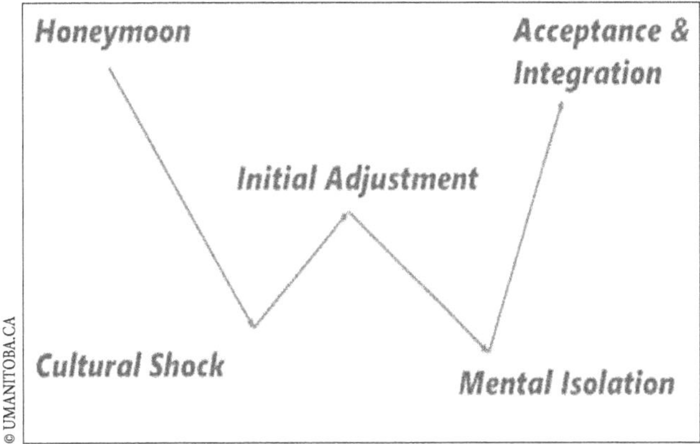

The experience of culture shock can range from mildly annoying to profoundly disturbing. It can be very pronounced in international students, immigrants, and people working away from home in international settings. For example, my experience with culture shock was so pronounced because I am an immigrant who studied internationally and later worked internationally in Mexico, Sierra Leone, Cuba, and Ghana.

The key to overcoming culture shock is first to recognize that you are struggling to adjust to your new environment. Then, try to learn as much as possible about your host country. Be curious about people, things, and places around you. Ask questions about the culture you are in and share yours too. Learn to manage ambiguity. You will not know everything. The learning curve may not level off for some time. Be mindful of ethnocentric tendencies and suspend ethnocentric evaluations. By that, I mean comparing your home culture with the new culture. Comments like "This is not how we do things back home" and "We do things better back home" may not help you transition and get to the healthy balance you seek.

Now that we understand the internal conflict that occurs let us explore how we typically deal with this as immigrants.

How do we make sense of the disorientation—the culture shock we experience during the highs and lows of cultural adjustment to find belonging as immigrants in an adopted country?

How do we balance the cultural expectation of being the fortunate few who live in the land that flows with milk and honey, supporting communities back home, and our personal aspirations?

How do we merge the sense of duty and responsibility that so many carry with the demands of a capitalistic culture and self-care?

Unfortunately, many of us become machine-like entities going from one task to the next, unable to be with the simple things of life like nature and family and embrace quietness, stillness, and solitude. Have you lost your connection with your "Being" nature that you knew so well in the former collectivist culture? Have you become a human-doing? After two decades of living and working in the U.S., I found that I was simply unable to slow down or stop the hyper-achievement mentality. I would go from one activity to another, seeking gratification, but those fleeting moments only lasted for short periods, and then I was off to the next task or goal. I became a human-doing. Here I am writing a book. This led to several episodes of burnout. How did I lose myself to doing? This is the question I pondered as I collapsed from exhaustion. As first-generation children of immigrants, this cycle can be harmful and must be addressed for a healthy balance of doing and being to set in.

So how do we slow down and balance the doing with the being?

How do we balance the cultural pressures of giving back to communities back home and our personal aspirations? Finally, you are in a place where you can seek out self-actualization, as Maslow's hierarchy puts it. The first step is recognizing that there is a clash and that it is impacting you. Secondly, you will need a community of immigrants or others having similar struggles to help you decode the experience. Lastly, if you do not have a community, seek help from a professional coach to help arm you with the proper tools. The clash between these two cultures can be debilitating and, at worst, traumatic. This is why I created a strengths-based interculturally competent coaching program to provide the support immigrants need to come home to themselves—to learn how to show up as their authentic immigrant selves and manage the cultural clashes between both worlds. The key is to come home to yourself. To embrace your authentic immigrant self, the changes, and

ATTORNEY · AUTHOR · JEWISH-AMERICAN · FROM BELARUS
EPISODE 2

You find it flattering when you are a kid, and you're entrusted to do things that all the adults [should] do. I had to start translating for my mom at age 12. When we moved, I would be the one calling the companies to change over the address. That was flattering for a while. Eventually, some resentment was probably building. I got tired kind of early. You felt like the pressure was on you. Very rarely it would be spoken of. It was kind of unspoken. Whenever I made the right decision, I would be rewarded. I was conditioned to follow a certain path. They wanted the best for me. It was all from good intentions. For a while, I stalled. I couldn't figure out what to do with myself. It was arrested development. It took me a while to find myself again. When I had my own kids, the resentment started melting away because I started to understand that, as a parent, sometimes it is unconscious. For a while, there was some resentment and stagnation. It was kind of a rebellion. The growing up is accelerated—their expectations of you at a younger age. 'You can do what you want after you do these serious things,' Dad said.

Lines get really blurred, and you forget that you are a separate person and have some choices. Figuring out who I am, separate from the group. I was the family and community translator. Anything remotely legal, they would come to me. You are expected to do that. I had to start slowly building boundaries. Potentially, some reverse resentment from the parents: why are you not keeping up with the community's expectations? It's an ebb and flow. Recognize that you don't have to fulfill that. There can be slights if you do not. There was so much intrusion from others, and it took a while to shake off. Many people talked me out of being a history teacher and into being a lawyer. I passed the bar, but my heart was not in it.

the hybrid of both cultures you are becoming. My own journey has shown that it can be a painful but necessary evolutionary process.

Now that we understand the danger of becoming a human-doing and the cultural clash between collectivist and individualistic cultures, let us talk about ways to balance assimilation, accommodation, and authenticity to achieve a healthy integration and balance of cultural dynamics and embrace *Coming Home to Ourselves*.

It is said that the Western world is where people come to forget who they are. As immigrants, we are told we must assimilate, but the assimilation target is often not clearly defined or is shapeshifting. Culture shock leaves us disoriented. How do we successfully balance assimilation, accommodation, and authenticity to integrate the collectivist and individualistic cultural dynamic? Lately, there is much to do about doing away with the idea of code-switching—which basically means adjusting yourself to your audience and/or environment. While this may be necessary for some groups, it may not prove pragmatic for immigrants. Therefore, I recommend contextual code-switching, where you tailor your authentic self to an audience or environment. For example, present a different version of yourself with family, friends, coworkers, etc. To do this, one must keenly know oneself. This means wholly embracing who you are as an immigrant (your heritage, your accent, your skin complexion, your curves or no curves—all of it), the value you bring, and knowledge of the culture and norms in the new country. Please do not give up your power to biases and labels. Stand firmly in who you are and influence from there. This is essential to building rapport and becoming a bridge person in the new country. Not everyone will understand the nuances of your former culture, and you will not know everything about the new country right away. Yet belonging is a fundamental need, a yearning to be connected, accepted, and valued.

The key to belonging in your adopted country is coming home to yourself. Coming home to yourself involves self-discovery, self-acceptance, and embracing one's authenticity. For immigrants, this journey often intertwines with adapting to a new environment while staying true to one's roots. Coming home is about finding a sense of belonging within, irrespective of external circumstances or the country where you find yourself. For me (and I can imagine for many of you reading this book), finding a sense of belonging in my new country has been a painful yet rewarding journey. Unless you live in an enclave around your fellow countrymen, it can feel like you are constantly shapeshifting to fit into the many expectations of the new country and your former culture. You are not quite like the former culture but are not fully accepted into the new one either.

Finding belonging is not a static destination but a dynamic, ongoing process. As immigrants, to achieve a sense of belonging in your new country, it is imperative that you build a support network. Embrace who you are becoming while making room to learn and adapt to the new world. Develop a system to accommodate the new culture while celebrating your cultural heritage. Recognize that the true home is often found within yourself. In fact, those of us who are hybrids of the collectivist and individualistic cultures known as **Third-Culture People (TCP)** have a superpower that many do not. We have the ability to see things that others do not. We see the value in self-care and achievements but also recognize the needs of others and our ability to make a difference and have a social impact. Embrace who you are becoming. Embrace your superpower.

Balancing the weight of expectations with the pursuit of personal fulfillment is emblematic of the immigrant experience. Recently, I discussed this balancing act with one of my former college mates, who is also an immigrant. We pondered questions about our identities.

How are we becoming more 'American' and what parts of us were still part of our birth culture?

We discussed the struggle of this idea of duty and whether there was space for passion and joy in the immigrant experience. As first-generation immigrants, we tried to be the perfect children our parents wanted, studied hard, and had less fun. He mentioned a former college mate who reminded him that he would frequently say that he had to study when they invited him out for a drink or some party. This was also me. I would respond, "I had classes, work, dinner," and take off to do my homework in some corner of campus. I did not have the luxury of failing classes or honestly did not want to fail. Finishing and being successful was important to me, so we both sacrificed college revelry for being responsible. Today, we both look back and wonder if we should have played more. We both have achieved a lot but are just coming home to ourselves. He, a successful economist and data analyst, is now doing live comedy shows, and it took his grandma's passing to realize that he needed to start joyfully living and doing the things in his heart.

What is the American Dream?

Many immigrants flock to the U.S. and other countries such as Canada, the UK, and elsewhere to make it big for themselves, their families, and their communities back home.

As illustrated by the voices of immigrants, this Dream encompasses not only individual aspirations but also a shared vision of community and connection. In the following excerpt by Marina Raydun, we hear from someone who has faced systemic abuse yet found strength in the diversity that America offers. Her experience underscores the power of cross-cultural relationships and the potential for unity among those from different backgrounds. By embracing our differences, we can build a richer, more vibrant society.

ATTORNEY · AUTHOR · JEWISH-AMERICAN · FROM BELARUS
EPISODE 121

It is amazing what systemic abuse does to you. You internalize it. Still, to this day, I do not describe myself as Russian. I am a Jew. If you forgot, someone would remind you. In America, I was looking forward to the diversity because in Russia, I was not Slavic. When people ask me what the American Dream is—diversity is one of them. When I went to school, everyone looked different. That was my American Dream. One of my very first friends was a Black girl from France. We did not even share a common language, but we would hang together. We looked different. It is strange that today, that is frowned upon.

No matter where we are from, as immigrants, there are so many common denominators and common experiences. That, to me, is empowering. That is America. The way forward is more commingling— more cross-cultural interactions, cross-denominational, and inter-racial friendships. That is the way we learn from each other. A lot of prejudice comes from fear; you fear what you don't know. If you stay in your respective corners, you never learn. The way forward is building more relationships. We have way more in common than we think.

The following excerpt from Tope Fajinbesi further expands on this idea of celebrating the unique contributions that immigrants bring to America. It encourages individuals to embrace their authenticity and stand out rather than conform. The emphasis on speaking up and claiming one's space is vital in a country that thrives on the diversity of its stories and experiences. The comparison between cultures—where one must be bold and vocal in America—highlights the distinct opportunities for self-expression and innovation that the American Dream allows.

CPA · AUTHOR · SOCIAL IMPACT ENTREPRENEUR · NIGERIAN-AMERICAN
EPISODE 26

This is a country of immigrants. We should never forget it. What makes America great is the diversity of the cultures, the diversity of the stories, the food, the people, and the experiences. There is not a country like this. Do not try to fit in as immigrants. Try to stand out. Let people see your original self. America is looking for you. Be you. Be bold about the experiences we bring. There is room for it in America.

What makes you succeed is different in the U.S. In Nigeria, empty barrels make the most noise. If you know that stuff, let your exam speak for itself. In America, if you know the stuff, you had better speak up because you will not get 10% participation points. I was reluctant to speak. In America, I cannot understand how you can like your colleagues and lay them off tomorrow. In Nigeria, you would know the layoff was coming.

Don't stop keeping your focus on your dream. Don't replace your dream with someone else's dream. Don't let anyone project their fears, insecurities and their definition of what the American experience/dream is. Because your predecessor couldn't do it, does not mean you can't do it. The thing that holds us back as immigrants is that we start to assume the fears and insecurities of our predecessors. You are here to create inspiration for your successors.

Together, these perspectives illustrate that the American Dream is not a monolithic goal but a mosaic of diverse experiences and dreams. It invites us to redefine success, not merely as personal achievement, but as a collective journey toward empowerment, understanding, and the celebration of our unique identities. As we reflect on these narratives, we recognize that the way forward lies in fostering relationships, challenging fears, and inspiring future generations to pursue their own dreams without limitations.

CHAPTER 3

*America is a nation with many cultures
and many languages, and its strength lies
in its ability to harness this diversity.*

—Former President of the United States,
Jimmy Carter

Decoding America

The U.S. can be confusing and disorienting to decode as it is not as homogenous as many other countries. Identifying one culture can be an exhausting task, and this can be quite disorienting for an immigrant trying to articulate what is American. One may observe many pockets or enclaves of different nationalities in major cities; the rest are noticeably segregated among racial lines.

(a) So, what is America?

- It is an English-speaking country
- It has a capitalist economy
- It is a democratic political/government system. Some argue that it is a republic because the electoral college results determine who is president, not the popular vote
- Social norms include assertive communication and cultural individualism rather than collectivism
- The rule of law is highly emphasized
- It is a litigious society where people will sue you in a heartbeat
- It is a level playing field, especially for immigrants, where you can achieve the pinnacle of success. In other words, you can go as far as your talents and skills will take you.

Assimilation into a new culture, especially one as diverse as the American culture, can be complex. So, how does one assimilate into something that is challenging to pinpoint? Perhaps the reason why there is not an easily identifiable overarching American culture is that the so-called dominant White culture is made up of people from different countries who bring their cultural backgrounds and often claim "whiteness" but silence the conversation about their heritage or roots.

Some dominant cultural mindsets of the U.S. are:

1. The need to be right and the first to do something.

2. It is saving the world and everyone.

3. White is right. There are certain cultural narratives, some political and religious, that one would be labeled a heretic or enemy if one ever questions those viewpoints or worldviews. It is widely held in the American culture that one should not discuss religion and politics in polite company. Speaking about political and religious topics could easily create relationship rifts. It is essential to be aware of your audience and tailor conversations accordingly based on with whom you are conversing.

4. Free speech is integral to American culture, but that can confuse an immigrant onlooker. Political candidates using hate or defamatory speech inciting violence and other behavior at times blur the lines. Be mindful of conversations about certain religious groups and political extremes.

5. Comparison: I haven't felt as pressured to compare myself to others or as judged by others as I have in the U.S. Is this the capitalistic mindset and the thinking behind the idea that we are what we do or that we are as valuable as the value we bring to the marketplace?

6. Self-interest is highly valued. I remember learning this concept in under-graduate school and finding myself confused. It took me years to fully understand, and through some hard lessons, I determined that I needed to keep my self-interest at the forefront while immersed in American culture.

7. Big is better.

   (*Working With Americans: How to Build Profitable Working Relationships* by Allison Stewart-Allen and Lanie Denslow, 2nd Edition, 2019, Routledge).

Clearly, these dominant cultural mindsets shape how people interact and think in the U.S. Whether it is the push to be first or the complex dance around free speech and self-interest, these attitudes create a unique environment that can be both intriguing and challenging. Understanding these aspects not only helps in navigating American society more smoothly but also in fostering better connections with people from different backgrounds. By keeping these cultural nuances in mind, we can all engage more thoughtfully and build stronger, more respectful relationships.

The Model Minority Myth: A Double-Edged Sword

The "model minority" myth is a pervasive stereotype that casts certain minority groups, particularly Asian Americans, as paragons of success in the face of adversity. This narrative portrays these communities as inherently more diligent, intelligent, and culturally inclined toward achievement, often highlighting their accomplishments in education and economic prosperity. On the surface, this stereotype might seem like a positive affirmation of these communities' abilities. However, beneath its seemingly complimentary veneer, the model minority myth wields a double-edged sword, inflicting deep harm on both the communities it purports to praise and society at large.

The first and perhaps most insidious consequence of the model minority myth is its tendency to oversimplify and erase the diversity within minority groups. Asian Americans, for instance, hail from a myriad of cultural, linguistic, and socioeconomic backgrounds. To paint such a diverse population with a single brush of success ignores the stark differences in experiences among, say, a wealthy East Asian family and a refugee family from Southeast Asia. This erasure not only marginalizes those who do not fit the stereotype but also obscures the unique challenges and struggles many within the community face.

Moreover, the model minority myth imposes immense pressure on individuals within these groups to conform to the unrealistic expectations it sets forth. The stereotype becomes a burden, compelling people to meet an idealized standard of success. Those who fall short often grapple with feelings of inadequacy, anxiety, and even depression. The pressure to excel academically or professionally, to embody a relentless work ethic, and to maintain a flawless image can lead to severe mental health consequences as individuals struggle to reconcile their realities with the mythic narrative imposed upon them.

Beyond its impact on those it directly stereotypes, the model minority myth also perpetuates racial divides and exacerbates tensions between different minority communities. By holding up one group as a "success story," the myth subtly suggests that systemic racism and discrimination are mere obstacles that can be easily overcome through hard work and perseverance. This implication is not only false but also harmful, as it undermines the legitimate struggles of other minority groups and fosters resentment and division. The myth becomes a tool used to invalidate the experiences of marginalized communities, driving a wedge between groups that, in reality, share common challenges in the face of systemic inequality.

Furthermore, the model minority myth minimizes the reality of racism by suggesting that it is a surmountable challenge rather than a deeply entrenched societal issue. This narrative overlooks the structural barriers and discrimination that continue to affect all minority groups, including those held up as "models." By focusing on the supposed success of one group, the myth deflects attention from the pervasive inequalities that persist in education, employment, and social mobility. It perpetuates the dangerous fallacy that racism can be outpaced by individual effort alone, ignoring the need for collective action and systemic change.

In essence, the model minority myth is a reductive and damaging stereotype that serves to perpetuate inequality and division. It obscures the rich diversity of experiences within minority communities, imposes unrealistic expectations, fosters intergroup tensions, and downplays the enduring impact of racism. As we seek to build a more equitable society, it is crucial to recognize and dismantle this myth, replacing it with a more nuanced understanding of minority experiences that honor the complexity and diversity of all communities.

While it might seem positive on the surface, the model minority myth is harmful for several reasons:

1. **Oversimplification and Erasure of Diversity:** The myth ignores the diversity within minority groups, such as the varying experiences of different Asian American communities. Not all members of these groups experience the same level of success, and the myth erases the struggles faced by many.

2. **Pressure to Conform:** It places unrealistic expectations on individuals within the "model minority" group to conform to these stereotypes, which can lead to stress, mental health issues, and a sense of inadequacy if they do not meet these expectations.

3. **Perpetuation of Racial Divides:** The myth is often used to undermine the struggles of other minority groups by suggesting that racism and systemic barriers are not real obstacles since one group has "managed" to succeed. This can create tension and division between different minority communities.

4. **Minimization of Racism:** By focusing on the success of one minority group, the model minority myth minimizes the impact of systemic racism and the real challenges that all minority groups face. It perpetuates the false idea that racism can be overcome simply by working harder or adhering to certain cultural values.

Overall, the model minority myth is a reductive and harmful stereotype that ignores the complexity of minority experiences and contributes to racial inequalities.

The Minority Tax: An Unseen Burden

In many academic and professional settings, individuals from underrepresented minority groups often face what is colloquially known as the "minority tax." This concept encapsulates the additional, often invisible burdens placed upon these individuals, which extend far beyond their primary job responsibilities. Unlike their majority counterparts, minority professionals are frequently expected to engage in a range of activities that, while valuable, can be both time-consuming and emotionally taxing.

One of the most common manifestations of the minority tax is the expectation to participate in diversity, equity, and inclusion (DEI) initiatives. Whether serving on committees dedicated to improving workplace culture or leading efforts to recruit and retain more diverse talent, minority individuals often find themselves at the forefront of these initiatives. While their contributions are critical to fostering more inclusive environments, these activities are seldom recognized with the same weight as other professional achievements. This disparity can result in a significant workload that is neither acknowledged nor compensated adequately.

Beyond formal DEI work, minority professionals are frequently called upon to serve as mentors and role models for others who share their backgrounds. This mentorship is crucial in supporting the next generation of minority talent, yet it often comes with a hidden cost. The time and energy devoted to mentoring can detract from the mentor's ability to focus on their own career advancement, placing them at a disadvantage relative to their peers who do not bear this additional responsibility.

Moreover, the minority tax includes the emotional labor associated with being one of the few or even the only, representatives of a particular demographic group within an organization. These individuals may be asked to provide the "minority perspective" on a wide range of issues, a role that can be both isolating and exhausting. The pressure to speak for an entire group, coupled with the potential for facing microaggressions or outright discrimination, can significantly affect their well-being.

Therefore, the minority tax represents a form of inequity often overlooked in workplace diversity discussions. It underscores the need for organizations to recognize and address the additional burdens that minority professionals face, ensuring that their contributions are valued and their well-being is supported. Without such recognition, the minority tax will continue to be an unseen burden, hindering the very progress that diversity initiatives seek to achieve.

These burdens go beyond their primary job duties and typically include:

1. **Diversity Work:** Members of minority groups are frequently called upon to participate in diversity, equity, and inclusion (DEI) initiatives, serve on committees focused on these issues, or mentor other minority individuals. While these activities are important, they can be time-consuming and may not always be recognized or rewarded like other professional contributions.

2. **Mentorship and Support Roles:** Minority individuals are often expected to serve as mentors or role models for other minority members, even when this is not part of their job responsibilities. This can create additional workload without corresponding recognition or compensation.

3. **Representation and Tokenism:** In many settings, minority individuals may be one of the few, if not the only, representatives of their demographic group. This can lead to them being asked to provide the "minority perspective" on a wide range of issues, which can be exhausting and detract from their ability to focus on their core responsibilities.

4. **Emotional Labor:** The minority tax also includes the emotional labor of navigating environments where they might face microaggressions, discrimination, or isolation. This emotional burden can be taxing and may affect their overall well-being and job performance.

The term highlights the inequity that arises when minority individuals are expected to take on these additional roles and responsibilities, often without adequate compensation, recognition, or support.

As immigrants, we must understand the system that exists in the United States. For example, business and integrity are not synonymous here—they do not necessarily go together. Hate or like it, capitalism is about expansion, innovation, and profit-making. I am often very shocked to see and learn of the extent to which people will go to get you to buy their products and services. There is so much noise that, at times, it is almost impossible to decipher a deceiver from the genuine. You must be able to spot an idiot. A few years back, I realized that many people are keen on dressing up their bodies, products, and services to attract you, but it is often deceptive once you look deeper behind it. The services and products are generally not to the level of what was advertised. They work hard to get you to buy and lock you into that purchase before buyer's remorse hits your consciousness. The Bible says that "God looks at the heart, but man looks at the outward appearance," which is evident in this culture. For example, some men will spend hours at the gym building their bodies (outward persona) to attract females, but often, once you try to start a conversation and get to know them, you realize there is no substance behind the chiseled body. They have spent hours trying to build their outward physique but less time building their inner strength, character, and confidence.

Another example is that small businesses will create quite the social media presentation of videos, captions, and stories around their brands. However, when you buy their services, you realize that they were not all that they were cracked up to be. Immigrants must be able to sort through all that noise, farce, and facade to get to the value, integrity, and authenticity.

Decoding the U.S.A. Political Scene

For immigrants in the United States, understanding the political landscape is crucial for effective integration and social participation. Here are some key points to consider:

Basic Structure of Government: Familiarize yourself with the three branches of government - Executive, Legislative, and Judicial. Understand the roles of the President, Congress (House of Representatives and Senate), and the Supreme Court.

Local and State Politics: Politics in the U.S. extend beyond the federal government. Each state has its own government, and local governments operate within counties and municipalities. Understanding the roles and functions of local and state governments is crucial as they impact daily life, including education, healthcare, and law enforcement.

Voting Rights and Registration: Knowing your rights as a voter is essential. Check the requirements and procedures for voter registration in your state. Many states allow non-citizens to vote in local elections, so knowing the rules specific to your location is essential.

Political Parties: Learn about the major political parties in the U.S., Democrats and Republicans, and other smaller parties. Understand their general ideologies, policy positions, and how they influence national and local politics.

Political System and Civic Engagement: Get involved in civic activities. Attend town hall meetings and community events and discuss local and national issues. Joining community groups or organizations can provide insights into the political climate and help build connections.

Immigration Policies: Stay informed about immigration policies, which can directly impact your status and rights. Understand the procedures and requirements for obtaining visas, permanent residency, and citizenship.

Media Literacy: Develop media literacy skills to assess information from various sources critically. Different media outlets may present information from different perspectives, so it is crucial to discern reliable sources.

Cultural Sensitivity: Recognize and appreciate the diversity of political opinions and backgrounds in the U.S. Respect differing viewpoints and be open to discussions that promote understanding and cooperation.

Language Proficiency: Improve your English language skills, as this will enhance your ability to understand and participate in political discussions, access information, and engage with the broader community.

Legal Rights: Be aware of your legal rights and protections under the U.S. Constitution. Knowing your rights can empower you to navigate various situations and seek assistance when needed.

As immigrants, you can contribute to the democratic process and create positive change in your communities by staying informed and actively participating in civic life.

Decoding the Daily American Vernacular Communication

Understanding the U.S. culture is daunting for a new or seasoned immigrant. After 23-plus years, I still find it disorienting to decode the different groups I interact with periodically and at any given moment. Many people in the mainstream lately have expressed the need for people to show up as their authentic selves and to do away with code-switching, but I have found that this is not realistic or pragmatic when dealing with diverse groups. I take a position of contextual authenticity when dealing with people outside my inner circle. The authenticity of this island girl is not a cup of tea for everyone. I currently host a podcast, "The Immigrant Experience in America," where I tell immigrant stories of triumph, challenge, and disorientation in figuring out this shapeshifting culture. I was inspired to start this podcast by my own experience as an immigrant-American who legally migrated to the United States but has frequent experiences of a love-hate relationship with America's immigrant population. I noticed insufficient recognition of immigrants' positive contributions to American life. In each episode, we share the journeys of successful immigrant Americans, how they navigated the complexity of being an immigrant American, and how they achieved their American Dream. This is a platform for us to get real and peel back the layers of what it means to be an immigrant in America. Our goal is to act as a bridge between cultures, providing insight into the unspoken rules of American culture and offering tools and language to help understand it. Here are some helpful phrases to help you avoid feeling misunderstood or out of touch.

Dog Whistle: In politics, a dog whistle uses coded or suggestive language in political messaging to garner support from a particular group without provoking opposition. The concept is named after ultrasonic dog whistles, which are audible to dogs but not humans. Dog whistles use language that appears normal to the majority but communicates specific things to intended audiences. They are generally used to convey messages on issues likely to provoke controversy without attracting negative attention. A dog whistle is "a coded message communicated through words or phrases commonly understood by a particular group of people, but not by others." (Merriam-Webster). "If you want to cast him as just a nativist, his slogan 'Make America Great Again' can be read as a dog whistle to some whiter and more Anglo-Saxon past." — (Ross Douthat, *The New York Times*).

Simp: a silly or foolish person. Urban Dictionary defines a simp as "someone who does way too much for a person they like." This behavior, known as simping, is carried out toward various targets, including celebrities, politicians, e-girls, and e-boys.[2]

A pick-me: "The type of person who constantly begs for attention and approval and has to make everything about themselves" - Urban Dictionary. A pick-me girl is a woman who obsessively desires male approval and validation, often at the expense of other women. Despite the word girl being used, the term pick-me girl is almost always used to describe an adult woman. The term pick-me girl is used to describe a woman who obviously and obsessively works to gain men's attention or acceptance.

---

2 Egirls and eboys are slang terms for young women and men who are active internet users stereotyped as emo-styled anime and gaming fans (Dictionary.com)

Shade: Shade is a subtle, sneering expression of contempt for or disgust with someone—sometimes verbal and sometimes not. The expressions "throw shade," "throwing shade," or simply "shade" are slang terms for a certain type of insult, often nonverbal. Journalist Anna Holmes called shade "the art of the sidelong insult"—wiki.org

Tipping in the U.S.: The culture of tipping refers to voluntarily giving extra money, or a gratuity, to service workers in addition to the stated price of a service or a meal. Tipping is common in many parts of the world, especially in the United States and other Western countries. However, the customs and norms surrounding tipping can vary significantly between different cultures.

Here are some key aspects of the culture of tipping:

Service Industries: Tipping is most prevalent in service-oriented industries, such as restaurants, bars, hotels, taxis, hair salons, and more. In these industries, tipping is often seen as a way to reward good service and incentivize employee performance.

Reasons for Tipping: Tipping serves several purposes, including acknowledging excellent service, showing appreciation for a job well done, and acknowledging the worker's efforts to meet the customer's needs. In some cases, tipping may also be seen as a social norm, with pressure to tip based on the expectations of others.

Tipping Etiquette: Different countries and regions within countries have their own rules and customs regarding tipping. For example, in the United States, it is customary to tip servers at restaurants around 15-20% of the bill's total. In some European countries, a service charge is often included in the bill, but additional tipping is appreciated for exceptional service.

Controversies: While tipping can be a way to incentivize good service, it has also been subject to criticism and debate. Some argue that tipping should not be an obligation and that employers should pay their workers fair wages without relying on customer gratuities to compensate for low wages. This is particularly relevant in countries where the minimum wage for tipped workers can be lower than the standard minimum wage.

Tipping in Different Cultures: Tipping customs vary widely across the globe. In some countries, like Japan, tipping is uncommon and can even be considered offensive. In contrast, in the United States, tipping is deeply ingrained in the culture, and servers and other service workers often rely on tips as a significant portion of their income.

Digital Tipping: With the rise of digital payment methods, some establishments have introduced electronic tipping options, allowing customers to leave a gratuity when paying with credit cards or mobile payment apps.

Immigrants must know local customs regarding tipping when traveling or living in a new country. It is important to remember that tipping customs differ greatly around the world. Understanding these differences can help avoid any confusion or unintentional disrespect. Researching tipping etiquette before traveling can ensure that you show appreciation for good service in a manner that is appropriate for the specific region.

Code-Switching: Cultural code-switching involves suppressing multiple aspects of one's cultural identity, including clothing worn, hairstyle, speech, or behavior. In the broadest sense, code-switching involves adapting the presentation of oneself in ways that disconnect them from their group's cultural or racial stereotypes. The goal is to enhance the comfort of others, typically those outside of their cultural or racial group, in hopes of receiving equal treatment and opportunities for advancement. Code-switching is a strategy used by individuals identifying as BIPOC, who often find it necessary to navigate professional settings effectively. There are multiple examples of code-switching, for example, when a person considers each morning before getting dressed for work or school whether their traditional cultural garments will be viewed as acceptable, whether wearing a turban, hijab, or bindi will be off-putting to their colleagues or supervisors; or whether their natural hair (e.g., afro, dreadlocks, braids, etc.) will be seen as unprofessional.

Code-switching also involves adapting other aspects of self that may not be as easily identified. In academic and professional settings, many in the BIPOC community are likely familiar with the term "Oreo." And no, I am not talking a bout the cookie, but what the cookie represents: black on the outside and White on the inside, the use of a "White voice" and other Western, Eurocentric ways of speaking, being, and engaging to "fit in" with non-Hispanic White society (*Psychology Today*).

Decoding Cross-cultural Communication

Cultural communication is the practice and study of how different cultures communicate verbally and nonverbally within their community. It can also be referred to as intercultural communication and cross-cultural communication. Cultures are grouped by similar beliefs, values, traditions, and expectations, contributing to differences in communication between individuals of different cultures. Often referred to as intercultural communication, cross-cultural communication studies how verbal and nonverbal communication occurs among individuals from various backgrounds, geographies, and cultures.

Some examples of verbal communication differences:

What does "Bless Your Heart" mean? "Bless Your Heart" is a common expression from the Southern United States. The phrase has multiple meanings and is used to express genuine sympathy but sometimes can be interpreted as an insult that conveys condescension, derision, or contempt. It may also be spoken as a precursor to an insult to mitigate its severity. Meanings range from sincerity to exasperation, primarily imparted through context and tone. Southerners know that when "bless your heart" is uttered during conversation, the meaning depends on the tone and context. Yes, it can be a backhanded comment about foolish behavior, but it is often a genuine expression of sympathy. The following interpretations are culled from *Southern Living Magazine:*[xxiii]

> A whispered Bless Your Heart: Can You Believe it?
>
> An empathetic Bless Your Heart: I am So Sorry.
>
> A sassy Bless Your Heart: What Were You Thinking?
>
> A pitying Bless Your Heart, e.g., "Aww, Bless Your Heart": You Did not Know Any Better.
>
> A neutral Bless Your Heart: I would Rather Not Say What I am Thinking.

"Yes Sir, Yes Ma'am": In many African and Caribbean cultures, titles like "Sir" or "Ma'am" are expected to be used as a sign of respect for elders and authority figures. This formality may be seen as overly deferential or even distant by some Americans who are used to more informal modes of address.

"Just call me Jack": In the U.S., it is expected to quickly move to a first-name basis, even in professional settings. However, many immigrants from cultures emphasizing formality, like Germany or Japan, and many other countries may initially prefer to use titles and last names as a sign of respect. This difference in approach can impact how relationships are formed in the workplace or social settings.

The above examples illustrate that the meaning behind words is not always straightforward—cultural nuances often shape it. Understanding these subtleties can help us better navigate conversations across cultures, ensuring our words are received as intended and fostering more meaningful connections.

Some examples of non-verbal communication differences:

The concept of time: Punctuality is highly valued in the United States. Being "on time" often means arriving a few minutes early. However, immigrants from cultures where time is viewed more flexibly, such as in some Latin American, Caribbean, or Mediterranean countries, might arrive later than expected, not out of disrespect but due to a different cultural understanding of time. This difference can lead to misunderstandings if not acknowledged and appreciated.

Microaggression: A statement, action, or incident is regarded as indirect, subtle, or unintentional discrimination against members of a marginalized group, such as a racial or ethnic minority. (Google Dictionary). It is a verbal or nonverbal slight that impacts people from marginalized communities. Microaggression was first used around 1970 by Harvard psychiatrist Dr. Chester Pierce. He used this term to describe the regular insults and dismissals he witnessed from people who were non-Black against people who were Black. He believed these experiences could significantly impact a person's psychological and physical health.

Types of microaggression: Microassaults, microinvalidation, microinsults. Here are some examples:

- "I don't see color."
- "You speak English quite well."
- "You don't act like other gay guys."
- "Can I touch your hair?"
- "That's so ghetto."
- "You should smile more."
- "You are not Black; you are Jamaican" (insert any other country from the Black diaspora instead of Jamaica).

Gestures and their meanings: A simple gesture like a thumbs-up can have very different meanings in different cultures. It is a positive sign in many Western countries, but in some Middle Eastern cultures, it can be seen as offensive. This highlights how nonverbal communication can vary widely and cause unintentional misunderstandings.

Eye contact: In many Western cultures, direct eye contact shows confidence and honesty. However, in some Asian or other cultures, prolonged eye contact might be considered disrespectful or confrontational. This difference can lead to misunderstandings if not recognized, especially in cross-cultural interactions.

Personal Space: In the U.S., there is an unspoken rule about maintaining personal space during interactions—generally, an arm's length distance is considered polite. However, immigrants from cultures where people stand closer together during conversations, such as in many Middle Eastern or Latin American countries, might unintentionally make Americans feel uncomfortable by standing "too close." Understanding these differences can help avoid awkwardness in social situations.

Patronizing: Patronizing behavior can often arise in cross-cultural interactions, where one party might unintentionally treat another as inferior due to their cultural background or language proficiency. This can manifest through overly simplistic language, condescension, or a lack of genuine engagement. Recognizing and addressing this behavior fosters respectful communication and builds meaningful relationships across cultures.

Here are some examples of patronizing behavior:

1. *Simplifying Language:* Using overly simplistic vocabulary or speaking condescending, as if the other person wouldn't understand more complex concepts.

2. *Excessive Praise:* Offering exaggerated compliments for basic tasks, such as saying, "Wow, you did such a good job just sending that email!" implying that the person's capabilities are low.

The preceding examples of non-verbal communication between various cultures highlight the rich diversity in communication styles and the importance of understanding context, tone, and cultural background in cross-cultural interactions.

In order to successfully decode America, immigrants must learn to balance the ideals of freedom and opportunity with the real-life challenges of social, racial, and economic inequalities. Understanding this complex cultural landscape is essential. Whether dealing with stereotypes like the "model minority," facing extra pressures that others might not see, or simply figuring out how to communicate effectively, immigrants need to be aware of the cultural forces around them. This awareness helps them find their place in society and contribute to the rich tapestry of American life.

Ultimately, America's true strength comes from its diversity and how it allows different voices and experiences to shape the nation. For immigrants, understanding and embracing this cultural landscape isn't just about getting by—it's about thriving and making the most of the opportunities available. By staying connected to your roots while also engaging with the broader culture, you can fully experience and contribute to America's ongoing story.

The America I Believe In

—General Colin Powell

I believe in America and I believe in our people.

They met in New York City, married, became Americans and raised a family. By their hard work and their love for this country, they enriched this nation and helped it grow and thrive. They instilled in their children and grandchildren that same love of country and a spirit of optimism.

I believe that our greatest strength in dealing with the world is the openness of our society and the welcoming nature of our people. A good stay in our country is the best public diplomacy tool we have.

As I traveled the world as secretary of state, I encountered anti-American sentiment. But I also encountered an underlying respect and affection for America. People still want to come here. Refugees who have no home at all know that America is their land of dreams. Even with added scrutiny, people line up at our embassies to apply to come here.

Later this month, I will be participating in a ceremony at Ellis Island where I will receive copies of the ship manifest and the immigration documents that record the arrival in America of my mother, Maud Ariel McKoy, from Jamaica aboard the motor ship Turialba in 1923. My father, Luther Powell, had arrived three years earlier at the Port of Philadelphia.

My family's story is a common one that has been told by millions of Americans. We are a land of immigrants: A nation that has been touched by every nation and we, in turn, touch every nation. And we are touched not just by immigrants but by the visitors who come to America and return home to tell of their experiences. (CONTINUED)

After 9/11 we realized that our country's openness was also its vulnerability. We needed to protect ourselves by knowing who was coming into the country, for what purpose and to know when they left. This was entirely appropriate and reasonable. Unfortunately, to many foreigners we gave the impression that we were no longer a welcoming nation. They started to go to schools and hospitals in other countries, and frankly, they started to take their business elsewhere. We can't allow that to happen. Our attitude has to be, we are glad you are here. We must be careful, but we must not be afraid.

You see, I believe that the America of 2005 is the same America that brought Maud Ariel McKoy and Luther Powell to these shores, and so many millions of others. An America that each day gives new immigrants the same gift that my parents received. An America that lives by a Constitution that inspires freedom and democracy around the world. An America with a big, open, charitable heart that reaches out to people in need around the world. An America that sometimes seems confused and is always noisy. That noise has a name, it's called democracy, and we use it to work through our confusion.

An America that is still the beacon of light to the darkest corner of the world.

Last year I met with a group of Brazilian exchange students who had spent a few weeks in America. I asked them to tell me about their experience here. One young girl told me about the night the 12 students went to a fast-food restaurant in Chicago. They ate and then realized they did not have enough money to pay the bill. They were way short. Frightened, they finally told the waitress of their problem. She went away and she came back in a little while saying, "I talked to the manager and he said, 'It's ok.'" The students were still concerned because they thought the waitress might have to pay for it out of her salary. She smiled and she said, "No, the manager said he is glad you are here in the United States. He hopes you are having a good time; he hopes you are learning all about us. He said it's on him."

It is a story that those young Brazilian kids have told over and over about America. That's the America I believe in, that's the America the world wants to believe in.

Powell, Colin. The America I Believe In. NPR, 2005
https://www.npr.org/2005/04/11/4583249/the-america-i-believe-in

CHAPTER 4

*The life you have led
doesn't need to be the only life you have.*
—Anna Quindlen

Culture Shock and the Clash
of Collectivist vs Individualism

The experience of coming to the U.S. has shown me how sheltered my upbringing was. I grew up in a close-knit community where everyone looked out for each other. The boundaries between who was a parent and who was not were often blurred because we all operated as a collective unit. As kids, we were disciplined by many adults within the community. I did not have to seek friendships outside our extended family, although I naturally had many organically. We would braid or style each other's hair, help each other prepare for prom, and attend all holiday gatherings. We also celebrated birthdays and weddings and mourned together during funerals. Coming to the U.S. has opened my eyes to my insular upbringing. I grew up in a close-knit community where aunts, uncles, grandmas, and extended families took care of each other. The lines between parents were often blurred because we all operated as a cohesive unit, and as children, we were disciplined by many.

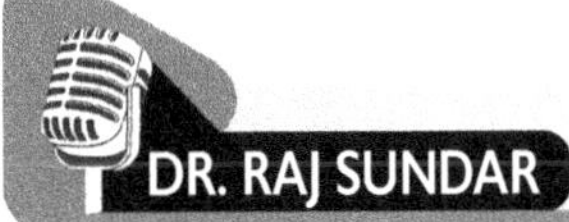

HEALTHCARE FOR HUMANS
WWW.HEALTHCAREFORHUMANS.ORG/
EPISODE 132

Many people come from a collective rather than an individualistic culture. People often hear the term but do not understand how it feels. It is like when you are a child, you have so many adults in your life that you do not know who your parents are..

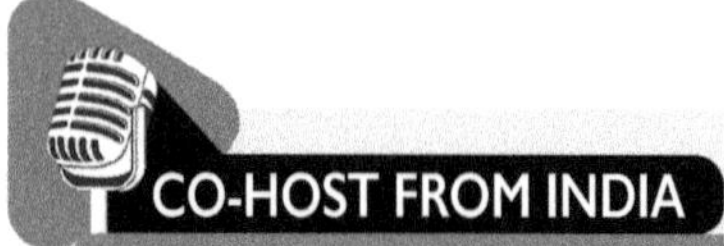

EPISODE 21

VISIT THE DEEP CULTURE PODCAST AT: HTTPS://JAPANINTERCULTURAL.ORG/PODCAST-2/

I felt angry with my parents too because they did not defend me, their daughter, in front of my grandfather. It was a revelation to me how my parents avoided conflict in the presence of my grandparents as if they were not in control of their own household. I realized that they, too, had to follow the expectations of others. They, too, had to fit into a larger world beyond their control. You learn that everyone has a position or a place in society and that respecting that maintains peace. These pre-determined roles give a feeling of stability. Spending time discussing or questioning is a luxury that is better avoided.

Ours was the home where the community would gather for play, dance, or celebration, and this tradition continued when we moved to the U.S. No one had a conversation about racism in the U.S. or the social dynamic we were embarking on. No one discussed it after arrival either. In all fairness, this was likely because race was not an issue in Jamaica. Our family did not have the language to talk about it. We grew up seeing dark-skinned people owning vast land holdings and living next to the lightest/palest of families. We observed them farm, share their produce, care for each other's animals, and live peacefully in a small town of approximately 250 people. Everyone worked together for the good of the community. This is not to say there were no disagreements, squabbles, or private networks. My family, for example, had a huge family and friends network across the island, made of the darkest skin complexion to the palest. We were always visiting someone. So, I know they knew little about how to have these conversations about race upon moving to the U.S. They were figuring out the new landscape with us—the younger generation.

I remember pondering about my skin color for the first time and what that meant in the new U.S. environment. However, I was too busy chasing my American Dream to dwell on it too much. However, after 10+ years, I noticed that my confidence was waning. I began to feel self-conscious. I was mindful of where I went, asking for a business referral and noticing that I was not invited to some gatherings. I started noticing how I felt in certain places and around certain people, but I did not have the

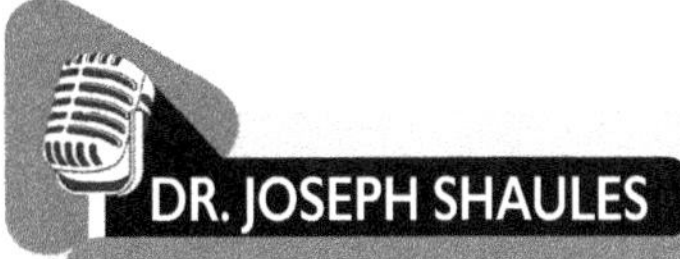

EPISODE 18

VISIT THE DEEP CULTURE PODCAST AT: HTTPS://JAPANINTERCULTURAL.ORG/PODCAST-2/

[Coming home to San Diego from Tokyo] is an odd feeling. It feels familiar, but it also feels a little foreign. I noticed things that I never paid attention to when I was living here:

- *Huge eight-lane freeways.*

- *The huge amounts of food they feed you.*

- *Strangers talk to you in the supermarket checkout lines.*

I sometimes feel like a spy. Everything is familiar, but I have this secret life apart from everyone else. I am observing everything that is going on.

__Co-host__: When I returned to India from Europe, I noticed these little things, too, like how people communicate indirectly in India. It is called re-entry shock or reverse culture shock. Spending time away from home even changes our perceptions of back home, and it is a reminder of how psychologically powerful a foreign experience is. We experience this often, more so when we leave home and spend time in foreign places——culture shock. This psychological disorientation is brought on by foreign experiences.

I just could not bear this foreign winter anymore.

When to shake hands or how to greet people and everyday interactions that wear us out.

Our unconscious mind must adopt new ways of interacting with the world and of seeing the world…feeling like a fish out of water. Your mind loses its bearings. Culture shock is a type of depression or mental tiredness. Our cultural batteries are low.

language to discuss it. I once asked older adults why things were the way they were at work, but they could not explain. I remember thinking, "This is not right; something is wrong here," but I could not quite grasp it.

I vividly remember traveling to Jamaica and feeling like I had walked into a warm embrace. The people were friendly, and the environment felt familiar. I instinctively knew how to navigate the culture, even though I had not been there in years. When I returned to the U.S., I felt replenished and joyful. However, it was not long before I felt drained and hyper-vigilant—in a state of heightened awareness and being on guard. Later, I learned about systemic racism and discrimination. I suddenly realized that my feelings of exhaustion and hyper-vigilance were correlated to these pervasive societal issues. This realization sparked my curiosity to learn more, and I began to listen, observe, ask questions, and educate myself on the topic. I have felt the sting of microaggression and folks flipping the table and gaslighting me as if they did not mean anything by their comment or gestures. The sad part is that some of these microaggressions came from other melanated people who phenotypically looked like me but were raised in the U.S. and had learned these behaviors and subsequently weaponized them against their people.

I had struggled for years trying to connect with people in the African Diaspora who would not welcome me in because I spoke differently, achieved too much too fast since I arrived in the U.S., was getting White privilege (told this by Jamaican male who lived in the U.S. before ten years old), was not black enough, and was acting "White." What the heck? What is acting "White?" The funny thing is that other elitist Americans, both White, Black or otherwise would consider me not proper enough either. This bothered me for the longest time because I was around many people, not necessarily around people from the islands.

Many people mainly focus on the positive and exciting aspects of immigrating to the United States and overlook the challenges faced by immigrants, especially those with darker skin. Due to a lack of knowledge or experience, immigrants may struggle with everyday interactions with neighbors, coworkers, and community members. This struggle can lead to a loss of cultural identity, feelings of isolation, burnout, mental health issues, and other significant problems. Finding a supportive community, which is essential for immigrants to thrive in the U.S., can be difficult.

Despite the impetus to assimilate, many gravitate towards the path of least resistance to gain a footing here. Immigrants often live in enclaves where they can speak their language, eat familiar foods, and practice their customs without facing

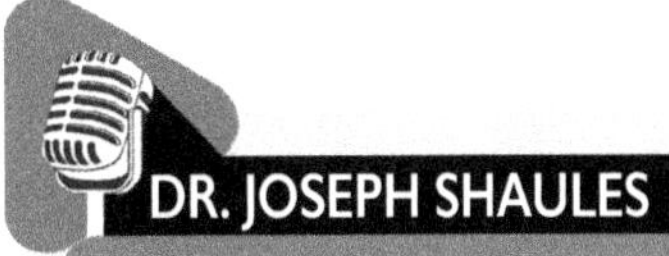

There was always one moment where I was totally fed up:

> *In **Japan**, I was fed up because the doors were too small and banging my head.*

> *In **China,** I was fed up with the system. I felt I had lost my individuality.*

> *In **Arab countries**, I was fed up with the people always changing their minds at the last-minute.*

> *In **Mexico,** I was fed up with the pollution and the traffic jams.*

Culture shock can come back anytime you are abroad. There is no permanent cure for it. Maybe with time passing, you just realize that it is just part of the cycle of adapting to a new place, and there is nothing to worry about. The experience of culture shock is different if the reason is voluntary or forced. The difference is vast. Culture shock can have serious mental health consequences. Symptoms of culture shock include feeling sad or hopeless, frequent crying, anxiety, lack of appetite, trouble sleeping, lack of sleeping, withdrawing social support, or even suicidal thoughts or behavior.

Finding meaning is more important than finding happiness. People like to feel good, so we associate happiness with positive emotions. Research into resilience, which is the ability to deal with adversity, finds that you end up less happy if you chase happiness. [On the other hand] if you chase meaning, you have more life satisfaction. This is so for intercultural experiences. If you start with the idea that you are going on an exploration, you are more able to turn challenges into growth. The challenges of culture shock or adjustment stress can be a chance to develop resilience, even if they don't always feel good.

the challenges of adapting to a new culture. This behavioral response by immigrants to a new country is human nature. We move towards the familiar, which comes easily and requires little effort. After all, adjusting to and decoding the broader American culture can already prove demanding. America is the place where many come to find themselves but lose themselves in the attempt to assimilate. The communities that thrive are the ones that can establish social capital networks, enabling them to conduct business, share knowledge, and provide support. Immigrants need a safe space where they can just be themselves without constantly feeling like they are under attack or that their mere existence poses a threat to others due to deep-seated fears of anything foreign or different.

I often find that when discussing race, the social construct begins to break down. People tend to use nationality and skin color in the same sentence, such as "I had lunch with a White person, an Indian, and an African." However, this can be confusing as there are White Africans and Indian Americans who consider themselves White, too. As someone from the outside, I don't conform to using my skin tone as the sole identifier of who I am. I believe I bring immense value to the table, which the stereotypes of one's skin complexion fail to capture in this country. I often feel exhausted trying to prove myself to White people in conversations. Many assume that just because someone is White, they are educated, well-read, well-rounded, and competent. This assumption is far from the truth. Perhaps if I knew their nationality or other identifiers, it would facilitate broader bridge-building or conversation. That is why I do not identify by my skin color. I identify as Caribbean/Jamaican American because that gives a sense of the culture I was raised in, the language I speak, and how I eat. It provides a general understanding of what it means to be Jamaican, although stereotypes such as whether all Jamaicans have dreadlocks and smoke weed do not apply to me.

I had a South Asian immigrant assume that I smoked weed because this person attended a friend's wedding in Jamaica, and it appeared that is all they did: smoke weed the entire trip. I once visited a former cotton plantation with immigrant friends from Latin America, South America, and South Asia. Both were horrified by the atrocities that enslaved people endured. They imagined I would be full of self-pity or anger, but I am proud of my heritage and walk in freedom. Not every person in the African Diaspora feels marginalized and oppressed about the past. On the contrary, we have come home to ourselves and emancipated ourselves from mental slavery, in the words of our beloved Bob Marley. Racism is a social construct created by less melanated people out of fear and desire to control. We do not need to adopt these limiting identities.

As an immigrant, it becomes difficult to know who is safe or unsafe. Some people will engage you in conversation and then weaponize the conversation or smile at you, and when you smile back, they swipe you with microaggression or a frown. I recently watched a TikTok video of a woman who had relocated to France. In the video, she explained her reasons for leaving the U.S., citing concerns about the prevailing sense of depression, hate, and fear in the country. I share her worries about the impact of this toxicity on my child's mental well-being, and I am still grappling with the decision of whether to raise our child here.

DISCOVERING THAT NOT EVERYONE WOULD BE HER FRIEND EVEN THOUGH SHE APPROACHED WITH FRIENDLINESS AND OPENNESS

…it was my first time learning Black history and learning about segregation and racism. I did not have an intellectual understanding of that, as I came from Trinidad. My major struggle with coming to America was understanding race relations and how they impact your relationships— and not being able to find deep, intimate connections outside of the Black community. We tend to come into the U.S. a bit more open-minded and inclusive. We can be friends with anybody, whether red or yellow or Black or White. We will be friends with the White people, all the people. And then you realize they may not want to be friends with you. I did not know that until ten years later. My breaking point was in 2016. I think that was the first time that I felt unsafe being in America because I felt bad that people were willing to overlook racism and bigotry. They were willing to overlook xenophobia. They were willing to overlook all of these things. And then that [would lead to] you abusing me because I was Black; we [would be] overlooked. My family [would be] overlooked. My husband [would be] overlooked. My Black child [would be] overlooked. That, for me, [hit] deep in my heart. I felt this in my core, and I felt really sad. I felt hurt.

TECHNOLOGY PROFESSIONAL AND CEO OF STREAMTRAIN
EPISODE 5

I didn't come here with any bias, …with racial bias against any particular group of people. I come from a country where our motto is out of many one people. We are a rainbow of people who love each other. We get along. So, you enter with that mindset. I never even thought about racism for a minute. The first time it hit me that people would judge without even knowing me was when my husband and I were buying our first home. Sadly, we found out from the realtor that because we were going to be the first people of color in the neighborhood, some of our neighbors did not want us to buy the home. Realizing that was disconcerting. I was hurt. I was excited about the [job] opportunity. I prepared myself. I can afford the house, but people would make that judgment just because of who we are [without even knowing us]. We just had to figure out how to navigate that. We still bought the house and decided we liked the house, and this is where we would live. We had to educate our children about the realities of living in America as people of color. The conversations we've had to have with our children because of living in America are not conversations we would have had if they were living in Jamaica. We did not have to deal with that level of bias. Now, I have gotten accustomed to the realities of living in America as a person of color. I don't own people's biases. If they are biased against me, that is not my problem to own. That is part of the sadness of the American dynamic for people of color.

Assimilation, Accommodation, and Authenticity While Finding Belonging

A kind of disorientation occurs for someone from a collectivist culture where self-promotion and uniqueness clash with interdependence, humility, and connectedness. Dora grew up in an East Asian country and later moved to the U.S. for an undergraduate degree. Dora found that she struggled with being assertive in class and speaking up to earn the participation credits. As Dora was interested in

EPISODE 22

VISIT THE DEEP CULTURE PODCAST AT: HTTPS://JAPANINTERCULTURAL.ORG/PODCAST-2/

Is maintaining a sense of self/cultural self while undergoing an intercultural experience possible?

How could culture shape the self? When do you most feel like yourself? It is not the doing that makes me feel most like myself but rather the being with certain people, my husband, friends, and those closest to what I have lived through and experienced. My American students often say they are most like themselves when doing something they like. Japanese or East Asian people feel most likely themselves when they are with the people they care about. People in more individualistic societies tend to experience what they call an independent construal of self. The feeling that the self is separate from others and has unique qualities sets it apart. Contrast that with an interdependent construal of self when we experience the self more in relation to others. In India, as in Japan, people use honorifics to refer to the relationship of the self to others. In Bengali, it is rare to call someone by their first name. You always need to add an honorific that reflects your relationship with them. People do not just use the word 'I' for themselves. We always say 'we'.

running for class president, she struggled with explaining her qualifications and experiences, which qualified her for the role. Dora later explained that she struggled with self-promotion and humility as her former culture frowned upon standing out as a tall poppy. Upon entering the work world, Dora was passed over for a promotion because she kept expressing her achievements in terms of her team's accomplishments [the 'we'] rather than her specific contributions to the results/outcomes in her office. Dora struggled with loose boundaries and often felt burnt out because she could never say no to protect her energy and focus on her specific responsibilities and the cultural expectations of friends and family. This example from Dora illustrates the clash that often follows many immigrants as they attempt to adjust to the cultural demands of life in the United States while remaining connected to their former cultures. This experience often results in tremendous emotional turmoil, stress, and sometimes isolation, as people like Dora can feel misunderstood by both people in the U.S. and the former culture. People experiencing this clash would benefit from the support of a life coach, therapist, and other immigrants navigating similar journeys. It is the clash between adapting oneself to the individualistic culture and maintaining the connectedness necessary to the needs of one's former cultural self.

Deciding to Assimilate, Accommodate, or Integrate?

Be your authentic self or code-switch? To code-switch or not to code-switch is the question as immigrants try to modify their speech, appearance, or interests every day to fit in or gain acceptance. Lately, there has been a flurry about showing up as one's authentic self. I completely understand the many angles in which this may be necessary. For example, for African Americans or those deemed "other" in this country, who constantly have to change to assimilate into the dominant European-American culture, it makes perfect sense to create space for people to share their authentic selves at work rather than hide who they are. There is fear of not being accepted, being unable to find a place of belonging, or being deemed "not a good fit" due to their proximity or distance to whiteness. In this constantly shifting culture, it can be challenging to keep up.

If you travel to France, be sure to at least attempt to speak French, or you will not be liked or met with a warm welcome. Many people outside the U.S. speak at least two languages: their native tongue and English or another. The French people like you to attempt to speak French; they will speak in English once they see you struggling. They appreciate your honest attempt to try, albeit a weak effort. As people like to say here in the U.S., all the French and Spanish-speaking Latinos learn English. This is America, but the craziness about that is that most native-born Americans do not speak anything but English. Yes, I said it: there is a double standard. It has changed over the last few decades as I have noticed that some are studying languages other than English, but I would wager that it remains predominantly a few. Many people lately have been saying that they do not want to code-switch because they are not their authentic selves. Still, when dealing with someone from a different culture, you must be aware of that person's culture, language, and generalities to build rapport. At the very least, it is recommended that one approach interactions with at least a level of curiosity and ask questions. Communication is said to be the speaker's responsibility, not the listeners. If you intend to form meaningful connections, code-switching is essential.

Trevor Noah (comedian and author), in a keynote speech, suggests when to be authentic:

> Authenticity always…must be…juxtaposed with context. You will never be your most authentic self with everyone, nor should you be. Authenticity is context-based. It would be best if you were most authentic with yourself, and as those concentric circles expand/go out, there will be different levels of authenticity. You would be differently authentic with your spouse, your children, your friends, colleagues, at church, in the city, in the world, and so on. Some people are too authentic in the office; they need to relax. You shouldn't always be you all the time without context. It is important to find some cohesive way to be authentic. It is important to consider your surroundings. Adjust yourself to your environment. There are cultural norms depending on the space or place you are in. You exist in relation to others. It does not mean you cannot be your authentic self. You seek out where you can authentically be who you are when you are with yourself. Save your authentic self for the situations that deserve it.

Depending on the audience and context, you will have to adapt your authentic self to connect and communicate effectively.

My Overall Immigrant Experience in Context

First, I understand that immigrants moving to the U.S. primarily aim to make it big. Whether acquiring educational aspirations, growing a business, marrying into wealth, being the first to obtain U.S. citizenship, or being the financial catalyst to support their family and community back home. Immigrants arrive untethered to past harm, trauma, or abuse by the dominant group/culture, a privilege that marginalized groups born here do not have. Therefore, they focus on achieving that dream at all costs. Most immigrants know the U.S. is about long work hours, sacrifice, biting your tongue, assimilating, and remaining invisible—the end satisfies the mean. Most immigrants understand the social scene and know that to survive, they do the work expected of them and get paid because they are playing a long game—duty and responsibility above all else.

I understand that some groups who have been living here for generations may feel oppressed, may think that immigrants do not have their best interests at heart, or worse, that immigrants may believe that the social issues happening are not our fight. While that may have some truth, because most immigrants do not know the history of oppression in this country, one must juxtapose the goals we arrive with against fighting a system that we do not understand, were not immersed in, and just learned for the first time.

While it may seem that many immigrants go along with the injustices we see around us, it is not that we do not care, but mainly because we do not fully understand the roots of the issues or how to handle these issues. I was shocked to learn that the entire history of slavery was not taught and has never been taught in schools. In Jamaica, we were taught West Indian, European, and African history and were taught the good, bad, and the ugly of slavery in the region. What we did not know was the harsh environment that existed here in the U.S., and the harmful tactics and strategies continued long after slavery was abolished—aimed at erasing anything and anyone connected to Africa.

I often attempt to share that if the truth of U.S. history has never been or is still not being taught in schools, how would immigrants from other parts of the globe know any of this to empathize? The sad part is that we gain knowledge and context from the images, stories, and stereotypes beamed from the media and our firsthand experiences with different groups upon arrival and living here. Misconceptions about immigrants' intentions abound. For example:

(a) **Why would an immigrant enter a new country with the mindset of not performing well at their job or not getting along with others?** Seeking to belong in a new environment by building bridges with everyone is crucial to achieving goals such as supporting family, community, and educational aspirations.

(b) **Why would an immigrant blithely ignore the struggles of other groups and project a "me first" attitude?** Imagine being in the shoes of an immigrant: You arrive in a new country with bright eyes, hope, and unburdened about the past. You desire to build bridges with whoever you need to, giving your energy and adding value to American society. However, you might be oblivious or naive to the struggles faced by long-established communities. Empathy and dialogue can bridge these gaps.

(c) **Why do some immigrants set out to be 'destructive' or controversial?** While newcomers bring fresh energy and ideas, they face choices like everyone else. Some become activists, advocating for change and justice. Others prioritize assimilation, adapting to local norms, and adhering to "When in Rome, do as the Romans do." Both paths are valid. Let us celebrate the richness of diverse perspectives.

My Immigrant-Mom Experience

FMRI research has shown that when Chinese people think about their mothers, their brains light up as if they were thinking about themselves. In contrast, when Americans think about their mothers, their brains light up as if thinking about a stranger. From an American perspective, it might sound like the Chinese or people from collectivist cultures are not independent. However, from the Chinese and collectivist perspective, it may sound like Americans do not love their mothers.

—*Deep Culture* podcast

I vividly remember, as I began my American journey, being very aware that I never wanted to have and raise children in the U.S. Well, here I am, raising a daughter in this complex and, at times, toxic environment for someone of African descent. I find myself being extra vigilant when dropping my daughter off at daycare, constantly listening and watching for any concerning behaviors. I started our little one in Montessori education because it was the most organic way to learn and experience the world. I certainly did not want to transfer any indoctrination that did not serve me or could come from others to our daughter. I wanted her to develop a fresh, experiential perspective of the world and people. So, we embarked on making the best of this world despite the apparent internal resistance. I was ready to move back to my home country, but my former teachers and friends would advise against it by saying:

> "Simone, get your money right and return later in life."
>
> "Jamaica would be an interesting place to decode after you have been away for years."
>
> "The economy has changed since you were here as a young girl."
>
> "Social settings and environments have changed since you left."
>
> "The media/cable TV has infiltrated the culture, and U.S. fast food restaurants are abundant in major cities."

So, I reluctantly stayed put and embarked on making sense and learning how to thrive in the U.S. I imagine many other immigrants feel the same way when they face seemingly insurmountable obstacles or just long for the simplicity of not having to decode anything. To just 'be.'

I could tell that our daughter was picking up negative and conflicting messages, and we were careful not to expose her to too much screen time, especially on YouTube, where anyone could post anything they wanted. It became a battle as we both worked full-time and would find ourselves exhausted from all we were doing.

One day this past summer, my daughter said:

"Mommy, I want to be the color I was as a baby."

I asked, "What do you mean honey, Mommy doesn't understand?"

She replied while pointing to the palm of her hands. Emotions rushed my entire being. I did not expect to be having this conversation so early. I was raised with the luxury of being in an environment with people who predominantly looked like me. I never contemplated skin complexion until I was in my late twenties if not my thirties. As I said earlier, I was raised in a bubble. In responding to my daughter, doing my best to hide the tears welling up inside and about to burst through my eyeballs, I said, "Dear, you are the same person. It is just that your skin tone changed because we were outside in the sun."

I could see in her eyes that she was not satisfied. I resorted to pacifying her by hugging and holding her for a while and explaining that we are born with an internal protection from the sun and other pale complexion people (peach people as she puts it) do not have that protection. We both cried a little at the top of the stairs. I had no other words; I just held her. She has always been a very intuitive child. From early on, she would say, "Mommy, you hurt my feelings."

Or "Mommy, do you love me? Daddy plays with me, so I know he loves me," and "I don't like when you do the interviews," referring to the podcast interviews I did so frequently for the first year of launch in 2022. I was unprepared to handle this kind of conversation with our five-year-old. I am still unprepared. Every chance I get, I try to pour positive ways of viewing herself and remind her…

…that she was created perfectly.

…that she is enough.

…that she is beautiful.

…that she is pure goodness.

Raising a son in America is another conversation altogether. I dated a young man who came to the U.S. at age seven, and to see the impact this country has had on his mental state after a few decades was frightening and sad.

I have observed many first-generation immigrant parents struggle to raise responsible, driven, and motivated children in this country, which is so different from the culture and environment in which they were born and raised. Many immigrant parents work tirelessly to give their children all they never had: the comforts, the access, the resources, the experiences, the knowledge, and everything else. Unfortunately, giving our kids too much often dulls self-motivation and drive.

How do we determine the type and amount of access we allow our children? Which is preferable? The previous culture valued community and sharing in everyday life, while the current culture emphasizes abundance, individual gratification, consumption, consumerism, and the pursuit of more and more material possessions. It can be a daunting task for immigrant parents trying to balance the flow of things while teaching sharing, community, delayed gratification, money management, and respect for parents that appear to be forgotten in the U.S. Many American children do not have to put in effort to gain the experience that comes with achieving something they had to invest a lot of effort into. As a result, they often take for granted, or cannot relate to, or do not understand, or appreciate their immigrant parents' hard work to provide them with the comforts they now enjoy. I have heard immigrant parents say that their American children do not appreciate the sacrifices they are making, treat them like an ATM, and lack the drive to (a) keep a job, (b) do their homework, (c) get out of bed to pursue desires, (d) initiate projects, and (e) overall have self-motivation to make an impact in the world.

My husband and I have jokingly asked, "Is there something in the water?" How can immigrant parents positively influence their children when they are raised in a different environment with distinct values, cultures, and beliefs? We often see children born in a new country with access to many resources, and their immigrant parents have set a great example by demonstrating a strong work ethic and solid family values. However, their children grow up to be disappointing, struggling to keep a job or finish anything. It is puzzling. Our only conclusion is that something in the food or water must be causing this. On the broader perspective, though, Forbes reports that children of immigrants fare the best in the United States in the long term. Perhaps we are just seeing the outliers from this norm that Forbes is documenting. We would love to hear what you are seeing and experiencing. The struggles are real and palpable for immigrant parents raising children in America.

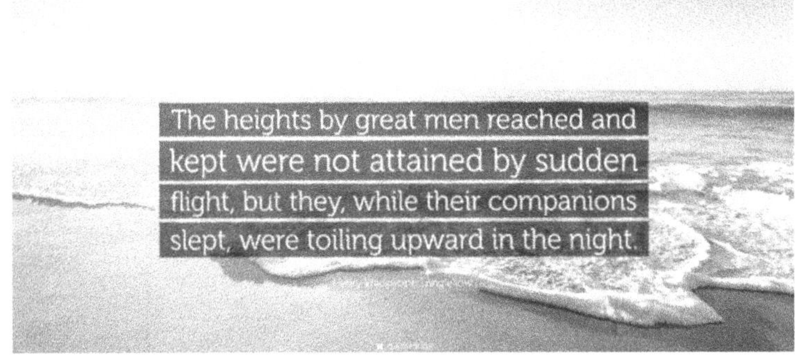

The culture of raising children in America is a concerning one for many immigrant parents. These are my observations, which are not all-inclusive or exclusive of other experiences. It appears that making one's children comfortable is the goal in this culture. Often, one can observe parents giving in to their children's desires or not teaching delayed gratification in this consumerist culture. There is stuff everywhere, and capitalism has made it clear that it will go after our children's minds and emotions

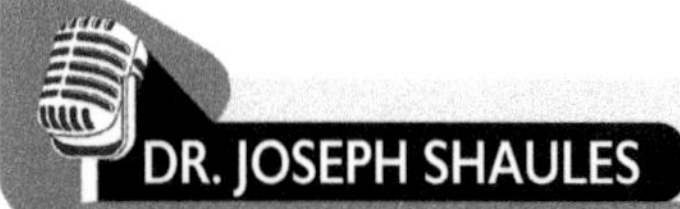

DEEP CULTURE PODCAST

EPISODE 2

VISIT THE DEEP CULTURE PODCAST AT: HTTPS://JAPANINTERCULTURAL.ORG/PODCAST-2/

In Japan, parents tend not to praise their children in public. Americans have this idea about self-esteem; children need to feel good about themselves to grow and succeed. Growing up in the U.S., I always felt like I had to be unique and explain my uniqueness. Adults asked me what I wanted to be when I grew up. What kind of sports did I like?

When I was in school, there was an activity called show and tell, and each child would bring some object to show to the call to share, and it felt a bit like showing off. Adults told me, "Look at me when I speak to you," and I was expected to give reasons for my opinions and tell people what I wanted and why. In school, I remember being expected to give a persuasive speech, and I had to write all these essays just to make an argument and prove my point. I got the feeling that you are nobody if you are not unique and can't explain it. The feeling I had, although no one said this openly, is that life is a competition.

Co-host—When I was a child, the last thing I wanted to be called was loser. That is quite a contrast with the Netherlands; they don't really like winners. You shouldn't stick out too much. This winner-loser contrasts with Japan. In Japan, there is this idea that the nails that stick out get hammered down." In communal culture, children are taught the opposite, "one of the biggest lessons I learned growing up [in Eastern India] is to listen in silence with a lowered head when being given advice from someone older, not portraying any surprise or shock and definitely not questioning.

as soon as they are out of the womb and make no apologies about it. The goal of advertisements is to influence this audience before they can give consent.

Parents often go to great lengths to shield their children from the need to work hard for something. Some parents will rescue their children from facing the consequences of their actions, leading them to struggle in the global marketplace and in education. At one extreme, some wealthy families pay for their children to attend prestigious universities. On a more everyday level, children are given everything and struggle to hold onto jobs or commit to anything. These children struggle to finish high school, pursue further education, and end up in low-paying jobs. Some immigrant families wonder how children born into wealth and opportunity fail to recognize their advantages. The audacity is that many of these families who have lived here for generations get upset at immigrant families for achieving more and make comments like "You are an immigrant, how come..." and fill in the blanks. Non-immigrants make fun of our children or our values or quietly despise us for sacrificing and being frugal. They say that those who laugh last laugh best. They may try to harm our children by making fun of what we eat, our culture, and how we live our immigrant lives, but guess what? In a few years, we will see who is laughing. They may try to console themselves by suggesting that we have been granted White privilege or that we 'brown-nosed' our way to success. However, the truth is that I refuse to engage in such behavior and could never bring myself to do so, even if offered a million dollars. I have worked diligently, studied hard, sacrificed leisure, and invested time to reach my current position. I recall being criticized for not wearing the latest name-brand shoes or clothing or driving a certain car.

Many are asleep in comfort. I never knew being comfortable could be such a debilitatingly numbing thing. After two decades, I can see it creeping in if I am not careful to keep it at bay in my personal life. Many say that America is the sleeping giant, and as an immigrant, I can see it in this culture daily. Many people prioritize their comfort over taking actions that may benefit them or their loved ones in the long run. For example, they choose:

- **Comfort vs. Health:** Opting for comfort—such as easy junk food—over healthier choices can have long-term consequences for our well-being. Balancing immediate satisfaction with long-term health is essential.
- **Parenting and Discipline:** Choosing comfort over discipline can affect children's development. Setting boundaries, contributing when necessary, and teaching age-appropriate behavior contribute to their growth.

- **Career and Challenges:** Staying in a job even when it gets tough is playing the long game. Sometimes, short-term discomfort leads to greater rewards down the road.

- **Marriage and Family:** Prioritizing comfort over seeking therapy or maintaining relationships can impact family dynamics. Investing in healthy connections benefits everyone.

- **Financial Choices:** Comfort-driven spending—buying expensive items to impress—can hinder financial stability. Making wise choices ensures a better future.

All these actions may bring comfort in the short term but can have negative consequences in the long run. In the end, balance is critical.

Immigrants make sacrifices and can be observed moving into different social classes, making financial improvements, and overall doing well because we can delay gratification and sacrifice today and live today—like no one else so that later, we can live—like no one else. Imparting this insight into our children is critical to their success. It must start with instilling the idea of being home with themselves without needing external validation. They must adopt the values of their parents and know who they are and where they come from—with pride. Anything else, and they will be lost in this culture. On the flip side, the following letter to an immigrant parent shows a different perspective—the child's viewpoint:

Dear Immigrant Parent: A Love Letter or a Wake-Up Call

How many of you have been estranged from your children because you treat us like pawns, here to please you and support whatever you deem your life's mission? What about what God brought us here to accomplish? We love you. That is what children do. We respect you. We even revere you. We see you. We see your sacrifices. You do what needs to be done so we don't have to, so we are one or many steps ahead. We are standing on the shoulders of giants. You often do the work in this country no one else wants to do for pay no one else will accept so that we can be ahead of you tomorrow.

We may not always know how to say thank you, but know your efforts have not gone unnoticed. We see the load you carry. We cannot understand why you are so tethered to so many responsibilities. Are you suffering from survivor guilt or have codependent tendencies? Being the one who made it out to the land that flows with milk and honey and has trees of gold. We know and see the pressure you feel from and for your family and communities back home. Though, we do not understand why you carry on with the people-pleasing, unable to say no or set healthy boundaries. Despite the obvious, many of it does not serve you and rob us, your children, of time with you. You are in a constant mode of striving. You are never present with us. The phone rings off the hook with calls from back home. We feel that you think we have gold spoons in our mouths and that we should never have anything to the contrary to say about it. After all, those people back home are less fortunate. They will never visit or live in America.

We should be grateful. But this leaves us empty. They say it is not what you leave for your children; it is what you leave in them.

What are you leaving in us? We have traveled on two different roads and lived in two different eras.

Do we have to struggle as you did to make you see our efforts as worthy?

Do we have to do things as we traditionally did to make you see that there is value in new ideas and ways of doing things? There is so much power in appreciating the lessons from the past while leaving room for a better way. After all, do you do exactly as Grandma and Grandpa did? We can never repay you for the doors you have opened for us here in America by leaving your life behind back home to start over in this confusing, disorienting land. So, we resolve to maximize what you have afforded us.

How do we shift this view of you as authoritarian? Our deepest desire is to know you deeply. To understand the road you have traveled and to know the stories of challenge and triumph. Do you desire to know what it is like to live in this country, this culture where you have never traveled before? Let's not waste the time we have for the lessons to be passed on to the next generation. We want to know your fears. We want to know your hopes. We want to know that you are proud of us, even if we never achieve another milestone. After all, when all this is over, what will matter the most: Were we doctors, lawyers, or engineers, or have you left the lessons in us that the creator sent you to share? We need to love ourselves and validate who we are becoming as we try to make sense of ourselves in this land where we have never walked before.

CHAPTER 5

Immigrants, we get the job done.
—Lin Manuel Miranda

The Immigrant Experience—Juggling Roles

Balancing motherhood, marriage, and a career is like juggling multiple balls in the air. It is possible, but not without effort and trade-offs. Many voices these days say that women can have it all. It is possible, but not all of it simultaneously. Is multitasking effective? Research suggests that true multitasking—performing multiple tasks simultaneously—is challenging and may not offer the payoffs we assume it will. Instead, we often engage in task-switching, which can reduce productivity and increase stress. I have tried doing it all at once, which has been exhausting. Even on my best days, when I am rested, adequately nourished, and in good health, running from one task to the next becomes taxing because that is the reality of being a working mother in the United States of America.

We do it all because our collectivist communities no longer envelop us. In collectivist cultures, extended families and communities provide support. In individualistic societies like the United States, the burden often falls on the nuclear family. Depending on your job and the work arrangements, your home often gets sacrificed, and your children have a very different experience of you because you are likely not present.

According to Stella Leaburn from *The Immigrant Experience in America* podcast, she would have had much support for her children if she had remained in Nigeria. Still, now that she lives in the UK and partly in Germany, she does it all for herself:

> The cooking, the bussing to activities, the planning, home care, attending to her husband, and managing her career/business.

> …when my son was born, I felt alone with my husband. Now, it is daycare and its cost. Then, leave your child with a total stranger. In Nigeria, this would never happen. The children would go to school, but there was always someone at home to receive or help the children. However, this is life [in the

individualistic culture], and you just deal with it. It was challenging not having that community that you could lean on.

It is hard to explain this dynamic to a non-Black person, let alone to a non-African person. In Nigeria, there would be an aunt or a niece somewhere who would happily babysit for you. Here, you are alone. You are the nanny, chef, chauffeur, cleaner, laundry, everything. Back home, these can be delegated, or people just take on these duties for you.

I, too, have walked this journey where I felt exhausted after a long day of work or travel to the point where I was not making healthy nutritional choices or having the time to make nutritious meals at home. This resulted in my gaining weight, inevitably impacting my energy level, mood, and overall health. Ultimately, it is about finding your unique balance, recognizing limitations, and making intentional choices. You are not alone in navigating this complex journey.

Some recommend the integration of work and personal life. Sometimes, home gets more attention as is needed, and sometimes, work gets more attention as required, but it may be naive to think that we can go hard at all times with everything on our plate. I went on a journey of journaling all that I had on my plate and removing things that were not as high a priority. It is God, family, career, and other things for me. This requires a lot of focus, being present with your heart about what is important to you daily, and applying the Pareto principle, which is doing the top 20% of critical activities. Coming from a collectivist culture, time is viewed differently than in industrialized, capitalistic cultures. I have found that my sense of time often fluctuates between these two perspectives. I often struggle with boundaries around helping someone or attending activities and events on time. For example, someone from a collectivist culture would likely stop to help a neighbor in distress on their way to work, which means this person would arrive late to work. However, in the individualistic, capitalistic culture, going to work on time is the goal, and the needs of others take a back seat.

I have noticed that many immigrants struggle with determining how much is too much. There is space for leisure, rest, and relationships in collectivist cultures. Life appears to be more balanced. Once someone moves to the individualistic, capitalistic culture, making sense of monochromatic vs polychromatic time becomes interesting—some struggle to be punctual. At the same time, others struggle to set the proper boundaries on communal expectations. There are plenty of examples of parents overrunning their adult children's nuclear families and extended families being too enmeshed in every decision.

A disorientation occurs when one leaves one's birth country/cultural world for another. It can take some time to adjust. This year, I have prioritized my personal growth and home life. I had to actively let go of things I had on my plate that were getting in the way of me being present with my family and doing the things that would bring me joy, for example, cooking meals for my family, playing with our daughter, and spending uninterrupted quality time with my nuclear family. I also released the desire to keep up with TV shows, comedies, and the like after 6 p.m. After all, our daughter is often away at school most of the day for five days. Evenings after school are the quality time we have with her during weekdays. This means I can sit with her at dinner, do an activity, or watch her choice of shows with her, have bath time and bedtime routine, and get to bed at the necessary hour so she gets her 10+ hours of sleep to be refreshed for the next day. This also means that I can care for myself after she is asleep in the way I wish to and turn in for the night at a reasonable hour. This has meant that I am rising fully rested by 5 a.m. with time for meditation/ devotion/ journaling/ exercise/ or something else with time to get her up by 6:30 a.m. Doing this has proven abundantly clear that I am a much better mom when I fill my cup first and wholeheartedly be present in the moments I am with our little one. I have observed the opposite: Parents are pressured by their jobs, keeping up with TV and social media, and gossiping over the phone, so the children are dragged along unwillingly. Both parents and children experience each other outside of ease and flow in a peaceful, joyful way. Perhaps waiting until I was mature enough for a family has given me the perspective and resolve that I had done the things I wanted to do before becoming a parent, so now I can let go rather than trying to keep up with the Joneses and everybody else competing for the time with my chosen family.

Another concern I have been pondering lately is what appears to be a battle of the sexes. I understand women's and society's history or *herstory* to some extent, making space for our aspirations. In the past, women were not allowed to dance (as I was educated by my daughter, who was told by her ballet teacher that the king did not allow women to dance), speak for themselves, work outside the home, and many more. Heck, that is still taking place in 2023 in some countries around the world, for example, in Afghanistan, where women are not allowed to be educated.

It is a privilege to be in a space where I can ponder the balance between masculine and feminine. I recognize that some women enjoy operating from their masculine energy most, if not all the time. For me, that is not the case. I need a balance of the masculine and feminine. I understand I am nicer when flowing and operating from my feminine allure. My husband and daughter experience me from different perspectives. Operating from a masculine place brings out a corporate bitch that complains, is never satisfied, seeks perfection, and constantly strives for the next achievement. My dear ladies, I have come across many of you who say that you wished you would have considered marriage and children while you were still in that season of life.

It can be a multifaceted challenge for those who have both a professional career and motherhood and must balance their energies as follows:

- **Dual Roles:** Women often navigate dual roles—career professionals and mothers. Both are essential, and finding equilibrium requires intentional effort.

- **Career Aspirations:** It is crucial to create space for women to pursue career aspirations. It is about recognizing individual potential and providing equal opportunities.

- **Gender Roles:** In a developed world, we must redefine gender roles. Men can be nurturing parents, and women can be providers. Breaking stereotypes benefits everyone.

- **Masculinity and Femininity:** Desiring masculine men is subjective. Authenticity matters. Men can be strong, supportive partners without compromising their identity as males.

- **Motherhood:** Motherhood is a unique experience. It does not diminish a woman's capacity for professional success. It is about choice and balance.

Ultimately, it is about honoring individual paths, fostering understanding, and creating a society where men and women thrive in their chosen roles.

How do we balance the feminine and masculine energies while allowing our men the space to operate from both? I have found that doing activities where I am nurturing my family, such as cooking, baking, cleaning and decorating our home, playing with our daughter, combing her hair, laughing, exercising such as hiking/ nature walks, taking dance classes or free flow dancing with our daughter among other things allows me to be softer. I am, in the receiving mode, flexible, adaptable, fully in the feminine. However, transitioning from a more assertive and dominant energy can be challenging. This can be a great challenge for those of us who are single professionals and have to manage our own homes, bills, income, investments, etc., before marriage. Nonetheless, taking small daily steps can help release the more aggressive energy and allow the feminine energy to resurface or be reignited.

The Mental Load Women Carry

Some time ago, a JCPenney photographer told me, "Women have eagle eyes." We see everything. You will likely know of a grandma or other woman who echoes frequent sentiments of "you've missed a spot," I am not sure if this is nature or nurture, but I will see so many things that need to be done that it can get exhausting. Men, it appears, on the other hand, can see one thing, focus on it, and be utterly oblivious to the million other things around. On any given week, I track our little one's school activities, emails, homework, school-related homework, my full-time job, podcast, finances, and many other things. I see this trait in many other women, too. Women carry a mental load that can be debilitatingly heavy. Throughout my travels to Latin America, Africa, the Caribbean, and other places, I often see women out in the streets doing whatever they can to provide for their families. I can also bet they go home to cook and care for the home and other family members.

How are we able to carry so much?

What is the quality of our mental health?

How do we find balance to release some of this cognitive load?

Most importantly, how do we solicit and garner our male partners' support to lessen our mental load? Do not get me wrong; I get that women in many developing countries find it extremely hard to do. The research shows that when women handle the finances, the family and their communities fare better.

So, what is the role of our men?

Are we to banish them to Mars and live among ourselves? Someone recently asked whether women would be safer if there were no males, and the resounding response was yes. As a daughter, wife, cousin, sister, and friend of many capable, responsible, and caring males, I do not see our men as enemies. They are our allies. How do we strike the balance as co-partners and collaborators in making this world healthier for our daughters and sons of the next generation? Throwing out the baby with the bath water does not seem to be the answer, as we both bring enormous value to the family structure and broader community.

Is there an art to being a woman or a lady? It appears that this culture has lost the art of women being feminine. Historically, it often involved grace, poise, and adherence to certain social conventions. However, today's understanding of femininity is more diverse and individualized. It is about authenticity, self-awareness, and embracing both softness and strength. The women's liberation movement seems to have brought us too far to the other extreme. How do we find balance?

I recently watched *The Bridgerton's* and *Queen Charlotte* and other 18th/19th century movies, which showed us how far our societies have come regarding women's rights. I do understand that women were viewed as property and could still be so in some countries/cultures around the world, but have we gone too far? How do we find the balance to be fully in our feminine and use the power of our masculine side, yet there be space for our men to be fully in their masculine (not toxic masculinity) and free to balance that with the feminine side of men (emotional/mental healthiness)?

Many women today are trying to balance multiple responsibilities simultaneously. I recently heard about a married woman with four children who gained several degrees while managing her family. It is hard to imagine the pressure she must be under and the hormonal imbalances she may be experiencing. I also hear stories of women who choose to have children while simultaneously striving for high-level executive positions, often spending just one or two weeks with their newborn babies. It begs the question: have we taken things too far? How can we find a better balance for the next generation?

When did it become a negative thing to want motherhood? I sense this general sentiment from some women doing well in their careers as if those of us who have chosen to be mothers have disappointed the movement, given into men or left the fight. Some frown on women who have left the formal work world to be full-time mothers. What? What kind of society have we become? Where are we headed with this mentality? Will it become fashionable to replace men in the work world and throw out motherhood? None of us wins when we go over the precipice of any issue. None of us wins when we demonize men so women can get ahead. I know some will say that I am being conservative or coming from a religious point of view, but ladies, it is simply being pragmatic. There is power in learning to balance the feminine and the masculine traits/potential in both men and women. How do we co-exist where everyone wins? Society is constantly pushing this winner-take-all mentality, and it has seeped into our homes and relationship dynamics and is destroying our families. Too far left or too far right is not the answer. There is a way to find a win-win for everyone involved. Our men are on our side, not against us. Maybe I am missing something, but I have had a father around all my life. I have had brothers, cousins, uncles, friends, and a husband. They only want to protect, provide, and profess their adoration for us. It can get lost in the mud sometimes, but at the end of the day, we need men, and they need us.

How do we find common ground and define the scope of work in our marriages, relationships, home dynamics, working relationships, and everyday life? Some men are bending over backward, trying to support us, but I am concerned about the Barbies I see around here. They want men to provide financially and head everything, yet they do not know how to cook, care for a home, and many other things that many women enjoy and traditionally do for their families. Yes, I know I have seen it. I have traveled across the globe, and I see it in Latin America, Africa, and the Caribbean more prevalently, where women carry the brunt of the responsibilities for the family. For example, they bear children; they are out in the streets trying to earn money to buy food, go home, and prepare food to feed the same children they bore with these men who, often, cannot be found. I remember thinking (I may have said it out loud), where are the men in Accra, Ghana, Sierra Leone, and Mexico? All I saw were the women selling produce or anything they could in the streets. I get it. But in the developed world, where the dynamic is different, how do we get closer to the balance that nature intended? I can hear the echo of some saying that we are blessed with developed world problems; we ought to be grateful.

"Let girls learn," former first lady Michelle Obama said, and I would also add, let boys learn, too. I am concerned about the wave of negativity pitting feminine against masculine, girls against boys, and women against men. There must be a better way. There must be some way to partner with the feminine and the masculine—men and women have both, and we need each other. How do we find the balance of the yin and yang?

Studies show that when women in developing countries handle finances the family and community fare better, and resources are managed better in women's hands. We are privileged to have developed world problems. Marriages are suffering because left-brain dominant women are finding it hard to walk in their feminine after years of developing and operating from the masculine energy. However, at the same time, these women frown upon feminine men. How do we return to our feminine energy and allure after years of operating from the masculine energy? The masculinity in men responds to the soft gentleness of the feminine energy, and through experience, we can use our feminine energy to spark masculinity in our men. Dealing with our men from our masculine energy may not be the most effective way to strike the balance many women desire.

Immigrant Experience and Religion

I did not grow up in a religious family; I only attended Sunday school with neighbors and a pastor who lived on our street. This is where I became aware of a deeper connection with the creator of all life and that it was possible to tune into that part of myself and live from that place. Church was a haven for me as a teenager. I went to youth programs on Fridays and sang in the choir. As an undergrad at my Jesuit University, I participated in a service trip to Ciudad Juarez, Mexico. During this trip, we built a straw bale home for a less fortunate family, and I fully immersed myself in the experience. However, upon returning to the United States, I realized that the perception of religion here was different. I remember having discussions with my cousin where we felt that religion was teaching us to separate from certain people. I also addressed the issue of missionary work with a pastor, expressing my disagreement with the idea that missionary workers go abroad under the pretense of helping the poor but with the condition that those they help must convert to the missionary's religion and adopt their way of life. These questions have always been on my mind as I seek to understand the role of religion in our lives. This would all collide as I attended a church, which I loved, with people from over 95 countries and found that I was building healthy relationships in the youth program; after attending on and off for several years while in the country, it was announced at one Sunday service that the pastor had a same-sex attraction to adult males. With no warning, another pastor read something in front of the congregation. The shock. The disappointment. Oh, my goodness. How did I miss this? This pastor was a staunch critic of abortion and homosexuality and brought in speakers on the topic—even one gentleman who claimed he had been delivered from it and is now living in freedom, happily married with a family. I struggled with this for years and still do. I realize that all humans have flaws and struggles, and I often wonder how some leadership in the previous congregation could have been more honest about the situation.

I have often wondered how the church in America is one of the most segregated places in the country. I learned that some people are only interested in interacting with me if I am Christian and think like they do. How is it possible to say out of one side of your mouth that God is love and created all of us but, in the other breath, express racist ideology or behave in such a way? One sees this in the Southern part of the U.S., known as the Bible Belt.

Belief drives behavior, which is apparent by some people's actions that a belief leads them to behave in a certain way. Do you know what it is like to live in a country where you know a certain population is hostile towards you and feel that you cannot call the cops because they are likely biased towards the perpetrators of harm? It is unnerving. As has been seen in the media in recent years, the law does not protect the lives of this group of people in many cases. It unnerves me to think about our daughter and what her experience could be as she grows up and interacts with the outside world. Some of the most racist people I have experienced are people who claim to be Christians, believers, and Bible-thumping so-called children of God.

The sad part about it is to watch older, 'more mature' church people of color, especially those in the African Diaspora, put their heads in the sand and ignore the realities of race relations. The worst part is to watch them hide behind the Bible, voice, and vote against their interests by siding with a religious perspective that undermines and harms them as a group. This is just too much to watch and digest as a younger generation raised around church people.

Religiosity is not personal development. I have had this realization for some time now. As I observe, many people are religious to their detriment. How is it possible to be in church, sitting and waiting for your life to change, but you are simply praying and waiting for God to work a miracle?

Dear friend, you must get up and act to create the life you want. God will not drop a husband out of the sky, a job, or change you supernaturally; you will need to do something. The Bible says,

"As a man thinketh in his own heart, so is he," and

"Faith without works is dead."

Why do you give up your power to a pastor who dictates what you can and cannot do? These people are to be guides but not the sole determiner of your destiny. Personal development means that one reads, seeks skill development, gives up poor thinking patterns that do not serve, and seeks out mentorship, coaching, or support to make positive change. I see this time and time again. Women sit in the church waiting for a man, but if they were to improve themselves, their mindset, and how they show up in the world, they may attract someone who mirrors who they have become. How will their lives change? Prayer is a powerful tool, do not get me wrong, but growth and personal development involve praying, meditating, and taking other actions to manifest the life you desire in this realm. In my experience, praying effectively changes you as a person, not that anything happens without you changing, internally and externally. Prayer does not nullify or erase ignorance

For many from the developing world, have you considered un-colonizing yourself? (*Uncolonized Latinas: Transforming Our Mindsets and Rising* by Valeria Aloe). Global dominant cultures have conditioned us to behave, think, and live a certain way. Is it time for us to think beyond conventional boundaries and consider what life could be like if we broaden our perspective to see the bigger picture of the world rather than being limited by the constraints of religion? I recognize that religious participation can be meaningful and lead many people to awaken to their life's purpose, or it can even provide a structure for self-growth or overcoming dysfunctional behaviors. Religion tends to bind us to a fixed mindset, though the Protestant ethic may suggest otherwise. It is possible to develop a growth or pragmatic mindset. Life constantly changes and often requires us to change and evolve to survive. I say this in the gentlest way I know how: please stop giving up your power. I have realized that every time I journaled about the things I did not want in my life or the things I did not like, it seemed to show up more. So, I started making affirmations about the life I wanted to create and manifest around me.

The Bible talks about free will and does not control your decisions. That means you have a choice. Again, I say, stop giving up your power to these religious fanatics and seek the guidance and power of the divine creator to manifest the life you were meant to experience.

Heart = subconscious mind.

Whatever you listen to and dwell on daily will become your life. Whoever can get information into your heart will control your mind. That is why so many media spend millions influencing your heart and mind.

Subconscious = hard drive.

Be careful what you think and listen to, as it will affect your subconscious, which is your hard drive. It will be running while you are sleeping and moving about. You become what you continually see and hear. Have you been struggling to break habits for years, finding it almost impossible because cleaning that hard drive has proven to be challenging? I have observed people in the church for over 20 years who have not changed or are still struggling with what was ingrained since birth.

Soul = integration of the mind, will, and emotions.

I have been careful what I allow our daughter to watch and listen to because the autopilot mind or subconscious is being set. Feelings, decision-making power, and thinking mind are in the soul. The soul is the mediator between body and spirit. The soul receives from the senses and deposits into the soul (mind, will, and emotions). Humans are spiritual beings who live in a body with a soul (Miles Monroe). This is evident when someone passes away. The physical body remains, but the spirit that brought life to that body is no longer there—that is who we are, yet so much of our world is set around our physical appearance and what that all means.

Whoever or whatever rules the soul (i.e., the subconscious mind) rules the person. Who or what is ruling your soul? Have you ever done things that you did not like? Behaviors within you that you cannot explain? Habits that you cannot break? Understanding this may help free you. The battle of life is inside, not out there or with other people. Have you ever considered cleaning your hard drive (i.e., soul, mind, will, emotions)? Have you ever cleared the cache of your browser?

Lately, I have been pondering how to clear my hard drive or clear the cache of my subconscious mind. What are you watching, listening to, putting in through your senses, thinking mind? Media means medium, i.e., to stand between. Who is influencing your heart and mind? After all that, let us put religion in perspective. Religion should not control you to the point where you are OK with killing another in the name of your faith. Have we not learned anything from past religious atrocities? Religion should not control you to the point where you have no agency of how to interact with others or how to use free will to go beyond religious beliefs and doctrine.

The Immigrant Experience with Nutrition in America— What Do I Eat?

Over the past 15 years, I have been searching for the best nutrition to regain the health I enjoyed in my younger years. It all started when I discovered my allergy to shellfish, followed by realizing my intolerance to dairy despite my love for dairy-based treats. It felt like dairy was in everything on the shelves, which made things challenging. Later, I found out that gluten was also causing issues for me. Interestingly, I found that I could eat various foods while traveling internationally without any problems. The COVID-19 pandemic prompted me to go back to basics. This is the story of my journey with international food and how it contrasts with my experience in the United States.

Recently, I have been reminded of the phrase, "Let food be thy healing and healing be thy food." Who would have thought there would be such a battle to find organic, healthy food options in arguably the wealthiest country in the world? Instead, we must wade through a barrage of unhealthy, processed, genetically modified offerings built to shorten our lifespan and vigor with our loved ones.

I used to be able to eat anything I desired without any issues. However, after moving to the U.S., I started experiencing frequent bloating and allergic reactions, sometimes leading to acute asthma attacks. This was often triggered by exposure to something contaminated with shellfish or other allergens. It is surprising because I grew up eating shrimp on the island, but now, I can no longer eat it or any other shellfish.

I have been on a journey to uncover why I gain weight so quickly. In 2005, after moving to D.C., I noticed that I had a lactose sensitivity and discovered almond milk.

That solved the issue until a holistic doctor told me I had developed a sensitivity to almond milk, so I switched to coconut milk. I loved ice cream and all things with dairy! It has been a journey of letting go of these dairy products and finding alternatives. I never knew how widely dairy has been used in processed foods until I was forced to read every label or pay the consequences. The food industry in the U.S. is an interesting one. The focus appears to be marketing to children and young people to desire unhealthy foods just for capitalistic gains. In the wealthiest country in the world, we battle weekly to find organic, nutritious food options for our families. I remember watching the documentary "Supersize Me" and realizing how harmful fast food is to our bodies. Those fries had a hold on me; it was as if they contained some addictive substance.

Whenever I left the U.S. for a while, upon my return, the first thing I craved was fries from a popular fast-food chain. It took me years to break the habit, but now I have been sober from them for over ten years. I frequently do a green smoothie cleanse to eliminate the toxic effects of unhealthy food in my body. I could feel fast food (especially from this same popular fast food chain) lingering in my system for over a week after eating it, and no amount of exercise seemed to help. Recently, I heard someone say that immigrants should stick to the way they were taught to eat in their birth countries. Otherwise, we may be prone to illness because of changing our innate eating habits to different foods and, in many cases, highly processed, genetically modified, less nutritious foods in our new environment.

As a new immigrant, you will walk into the general, popular grocery stores and likely recognize very little on the shelves. You may also get brainwashed into believing you are cool eating fast food, foods lacking in nutrients and highly processed. I have struggled to get our daughter to eat what we eat at home and eat healthy, nutrient-dense foods. She sees other children at school eating foods that mommy and daddy do not eat, which equals the eating habits of other households and other parents' poor food choices. She feels that children eat different foods from adults. We hope introducing her to cultural foods and healthier foods here will encourage her to make better choices as she grows and matures.

COVID brought me back to basics. When we could no longer go to salons or stores, I began learning how to make my own hair products. I was inspired by memories of the women in our family making egg conditioners and homemade items to support healthy hair, so I made aloe vera mixers, lavender, rosemary, olive oil, and coconut mixtures because I had more time at home. My journey to stop using strong chemicals on my hair began as I transitioned to organic, healthier options for myself and our daughter because my body appeared to be inflamed by many of the foods I ate and products I used (who knew that getting blowouts could lead to my discovery that I was allergic to some hair products). I had to make serious changes for my overall health. I started eating more plant-based products, doing green smoothie cleanses, and finding alternatives for dairy, gluten-free, shellfish-free, topical products with no parabens, sulfates, and other drying chemicals. Eating organic was easy on the island, but one has to read every label and chase down nutritious options here. Thankfully, there are options to buy directly from farmers and others who may use fewer chemicals. Everything on the shelf is made for mass consumption to make more profits, but it is not necessarily organic or nutritious. (Documentary: *Food industry Lesson: Let food be thy healing and healing by thy food*)

The Immigrant Experience with Finances in America

The overarching culture in the U.S. seems to use credit to the max to live the life you want now. Many immigrants adopt this mindset and find themselves buried in debt soon after arrival if they are not connected to a social network to advise them. In many collectivist cultures, where many immigrants are from, the idea of credit is not as widely used. There is way more red tape and obstacles to getting access to credit, but not here. I remember getting offers in the mail for credit cards, lines of credit, and more when I attended university. I remember that I would pay back my salary with my credit cards while working. After a while, I was done with the lack of gratification from that cycle. I would do my hours after classes as a bank teller, get my paycheck, and then realize I need to clear my credit card or face interest. Luckily, I knew enough not to allow the credit card balance to run too high. So, I eventually paid off the credit card, cut up the cards, and stayed with cash. This meant that I had to be frugal with the little I was earning. I could not buy the latest tennis shoes and clothes, go out bar hopping, or do other things college mates and others were doing. I felt deprived, but I had to practice delaying the gratification. No one directly warned us, but I observed my parents practicing healthy financial habits at home and always discussing maintaining good credit, which influenced my decisions. My frugal immigrant parents seemed dull then because life felt restricted, especially in a culture like this where everyone is trying to impress the Joneses even if they know no one with the name Jones. But thankfully, as I matured, I could see the wisdom in my parents' decisions. The sacrifices, the times they said "no" and saved us from ourselves despite the pressures from other parents behaving to the contrary.

Lesson: make sure to seek advice from your social network if you have one, use credit wisely, and make a financial plan to manage your income, including saving, because there are many vultures in this economy waiting to convince you that you should exchange what you have earned for their poorly manufactured products, service or food. You could likely end up penniless, indebted, without a roof over your head, or have your car impounded or worse if you put your head in the sand, impress the Joneses, and try to keep up with every fad or trend. Despite the social pressure, you can stay frugal. You will experience living like no one else because you delayed gratification, made significant sacrifices, used your time wisely, and educated yourself that you will end up years ahead of many who were born with the proverbial gold spoon in their mouths and in this land that flows with milk and honey. I remember an ex and others being shocked by how much I had achieved over a short period since arriving in the U.S. It is easy; immigrants and native-born Americans can make wiser choices financially and practice a little delayed gratification. Our society will benefit from it, and the next generation will thank us.

Boundaries, What's That?

Learning boundaries has been essential for my survival and health here in the United States of America. I was born in a collectivist culture where interdependence and community cohesion are paramount. There is no sense of self-interest. From birth, we were taught to look out for the good of everyone and act to please everyone around us.

When I arrived in the U.S., I continued operating like my subconscious/autopilot mind was set. I would travel and think of so many people to bring back little gifts for, as I considered them part of my community. My plate was so large. Over time, this way of operating exhausted me and turned out not to serve me. I was tethered to so many people. There was such an internal battle. I needed to focus on school and do my best, but I struggled with the conditioning of the collective. Pull as you climb. Give back as you earn. Help this one and that one, no matter if you are bleeding. Friends from that season of life could testify to how little I focused on my joy and making sure I was ok. The sad part was that the folks I was so concerned about did what they wanted to do with their time, resources, and energy.

Can you visualize two cups of water in both hands?

You pour some from one cup into the other cup. If you continue to pour from the first cup to the second cup, the first cup will eventually end up empty—no more water to pour into the other. The same applies if one pours from one cup to an empty cup without pouring back from the second cup

NIGERIAN-AMERICAN · CPA · AUTHOR · SOCIAL IMPACT ENTREPRENEUR
EPISODE 1630

…Immigrants are coming here with great plans and not knowing that America can derail those plans if you are not careful. People come here searching for the American Dream, but eventually, we end up chasing somebody else's dream. Developing countries can be bad, but America can be worse if you don't get your money right. It is important that we get our money right and we don't leave our plans to somebody else. I have seen how much of a trap debt can be in terms of trying to achieve the American Dream."

"I came to the U.S. on a plane, and I do not want to go back on a boat. A lot of lending practices target immigrants because they come and have been told about this American Dream, and they are working hard to achieve it. This is their chance to move up. Are you really moving up if you are moving into debt? You must have your own plan. If you do not have your own plan, you will be forced to fit into other people's plans."

"Money is a spiritual thing. It will fit into as much space as we let it fit into. If you keep thinking you deserve things, you will never get there. Separate your needs from your wants and practice delayed gratification so we can have an easier life for ourselves and our children. I placed a nuclear weapon on everything that I thought could wait. Are we going to be the immigrants who leave debt for those we leave here? This question needs to be answered in our finances. There are sacrifices we need to make so that we can have a better tomorrow. What is your relationship with money? Money is an emotional thing. The way we spend money is about how we feel about ourselves, other people, the way it makes us feel.

to the first cup. This is how energy flows. It is given and received from other energy sources.

In collectivist cultures, everyone is giving, all our cups get filled. In individualistic cultures, many take energy and give none back, some end up empty.

As an undergrad, I pondered the idea of self-interest. I had never heard of this idea on the island anywhere throughout my previous years of education. After years of pouring out and being around people who operate from the self-interest or "What's in it for me" (WIIFM) mentality. It felt like I needed to change and behave in the same way as people who prioritize the "WIIFM" mentality: come, take, and leave. I had to learn the hard way to consider my self-interest and the idea of "WIIFM" in this individualistic society. I am a natural giver. I share information and connect people. I share knowledge, and we all benefit when we give. It took some hard lessons to realize that this mentality is not shared by many of the people I dealt with. It was time to grow up and prioritize Simone. Prioritize my self-interest over that of everyone else. I recently took the Myers-Briggs Personality assessment, and it surprised me by detailing my personality as someone who looks out for the needs of others while neglecting my own. It has been challenging for me to learn this lesson, and I am still working on it daily. Setting boundaries with family and friends in marriage, business, and work has been crucial.

Codependency is highly prevalent in collectivist cultures. It can also be observed at significant levels in the U.S. Do not get me wrong, it is essential to share and live in a community, but when it comes to an individualist culture, operating from a collectivist mindset when others around you are operating solely from their self-interest and WIIFM mentality will not serve you. You will be viewed as prey. Learn to set boundaries regarding the people you allow around you. People who just come to take. It is okay to be altruistic, but make sure you fill your tank first. A well where everyone takes water daily will eventually run dry.

I have had to take drastic measures to stop the behaviors that kept leading me to emptiness. Pouring out, pouring out, and no one pouring back into my cup. If everyone drinks from your well, it will eventually run dry. There needs to be a stream or something flowing into your well that continually replenishes your well. In 2023, I practiced saying "no" to anything I could. I had to build that muscle because I did not know how to say no. I had to let go of relationships that were feeding from my well and spend their energies, resources, time, and emotional investment elsewhere and come back to replenish and leave again.

Slow down so you can clearly see who is in your inner circle. As the dust settled, I could identify those hiding in the shadows, speaking poorly over my life, wishing me ill, and simply taking. It was shocking to see what came out of the mouths of some people I was hanging around or with whom I felt obligated to spend time. It was heartbreaking. This is an essential lesson for an immigrant-American.

I was operating from a place of the collective mindset, but people only saw me as a thriving entity and that I had plenty to give, so they felt nothing about just taking and coming to fill their cup. People in collectivist settings are conditioned to support people no matter what, even if they would be completely irresponsible with their resource decisions. I realized that so many cared little about how I lived or what was going on in my life. Again, it is healthy to give back, but be sure to manage how this is done. I have decided that people-pleasing stops with me. Our daughter will be free of this conditioning. I had to choose to use my energies to accomplish what God has me here to accomplish. This type of behavior will keep you blinded to your purpose.

Guilt and shame are heavily weaponized in collectivist cultures to control people. Elders use it with their children, grandchildren, and others to get people to comply. Would you rather be at war with the world and at peace with yourself or at peace with everyone and at war with yourself?"

As for me, I have endeavored to reset my hard drive, clear the cache, and take control of how I show up with people. To stop the people-pleasing. The serving until you end up empty. I want to slow down to see what is happening around me. Watch out for people who come into your life to create drama—muddy the water, stir up dust so that you cannot see clearly so that they can control you . There is something called the *Black Tax*—where if someone is successful, they are obligated to give back to their community. It is likely in other cultures, too, but I came across this idea in my podcast interview with Stella Leaburn—handouts to no end. I did not realize until recently that guilt was underlying some parts of my life and how I showed up. People in the collective will use these as weapons to control you, so you continue to play the roles you have always played. Once you begin to change, they will send back messages that they do not like the way you are changing because it no longer serves them, or they lose the control they had over you. Walk in the freedom of the guilt that comes with moving abroad and becoming successful—survivor's guilt and cultural pressures to give back and the realities.

According to the reports "The Struggles of a First-Generation Immigrant" and "Why Is There a Higher Rate of Imposter Syndrome among BIPOC?"

64% of international migrants (58% in 2000), or 165 million persons, lived in a developed country. According to a Harvard University study, imposter syndrome is significantly higher among ethnic minorities. Escaping the grim realities by coming to a country with a land full of opportunities can often lead to feeling the survivor's guilt, wondering if you truly deserve the recognition you have worked hard for, knowing the community back home is still suffering through social-economic oppression or under the poverty line.[xxvi]

THE IMMIGRANT EXPERIENCE IN AMERICA PODCAST

EPISODES 86, 87.

"I share those parts of the culture with my children. My children are somewhat far removed from the [responsibility]. In some respect, I have contributed to that. As much as I do not mind giving back, I also know the kind of burden that it places on you. If anything happens, you are the go-to person. It can be very exhausting. Especially if you are the oldest or the one who has done better, then the responsibility falls on you. I don't want my children to feel that sort of burden placed on them. In a way, I have sort of distanced them from that. One exposure to the wrong family member and you become Santa Claus forever. You all get all that you can out of me because it will not continue with my daughter. In the last few years, I have started having firmer boundaries. I had to have [many] difficult conversations to the point where I stopped taking certain phone calls. It was hard, but I had to do it. It turns out that this person whom I was paying their children's school fees for years, I found out that this money was being used to build a second house. I was shocked…I had to start blocking people. [Now] I go to Thailand where I am not related to anyone. There I can get a break from packing many suitcases and relax a bit. That's what I had to do to keep my peace….

A lot of the time, they will try to make you feel guilty. They will try emotional manipulation. I had someone laugh at me because I had an iPhone 6, and they had an iPhone 10. Someone has got their priorities wrong. When you stop, they do not stop living. When you continue a certain cycle over and over, it is not their problem; it is now your issue."

Teaching people how to fish is better than giving them weekly handouts. I am not referencing relatives or friends back home who are genuinely in need and are grateful for the support. I specifically reference those in communal cultures who may not want to change or grow. They may prefer that you work hard in the U.S. so they can continue to live irresponsibly and immaturely. If you are going through a transition and trying to shed these behaviors or people from your life, know that you are not alone. It is essential to have a supportive community, distance yourself from these negative influences, and stay disciplined in order to continue your personal growth journey. You may be slipping back into old habits and roles without these things. Some collectivist cultures promote unhealthy behaviors like codependent love and fear-based giving to please others. It is essential to break free from these patterns and create new ways of living and being that are healthy and sustainable. Ultimately, it is about fostering resilience, understanding cultural nuances, and creating pathways for positive change.

It is possible to become a hybrid of collectivist and individualistic cultures—**Third-Culture People**. If you belong to this category, then you have or can develop your superpower. You see things others do not see. You recognize nuances that are not evident to people who may only have lived entirely in one of the two cultural settings. Use this to your advantage to create the life you were meant to have. A healthy, aware, growing daily, authentic version of you!

Achieving the American Dream: The Expectation of Making It Big in America. Is It Realistic?

The stories are abundant of people who come to America to work to support family and community. These sacrificial lambs or fortunate few give to the greatest extent. They are working two, three, or more jobs with extended periods of poor sleep, little self-care, and extreme behaviors that are not innate to the cultures they were born in (specifically collectivist cultures). First-generation immigrants face challenges such as poor mental health, language barriers, a search for belonging, lack of resources, carving out their own path without any guidance, supporting everyone back home, the feeling of not truly belonging anywhere, the silent uphill battles, the constant self-doubt and survivor guilt.

I once heard of a young Indian man who committed suicide at a well-known university and a lady who had sacrificed her entire life to work and send support back home. She became ill and finally went home to enjoy the fruits of her labor but could not. She later died, leaving it all. So, I ask you? Is it worth it?

How are you balancing the demands and responsibilities of your families and communities back home?

What self-care regimen do you practice daily to ensure you are healthy enough to do what so many want you to do?

Do you make time for yourself to rest, prepare nutritious meals, seek the appropriate medical support, insulate yourself against racism, prejudice, accent, and other biases, seek mental health support, find a community of your countrymen/women to be in a place where you can be your authentic self without the constant code-switching and assimilation requirements of your new culture, a place where you are accepted for who you are, a place of belonging?

Will you be one of those who sacrifice and work yourself to death to support your family and your community back home?

Will the immigrant survivor's guilt drive you to an early grave?

It is possible to balance the doing, the giving, the sacrificing, the trauma, and the toll of your adopted country, but you must be deliberate in taking action to soften the blows. The rhythm of life in an industrialized country is unlike any developing, collectivist country. There are changes in weather patterns (snow, cold temperatures, darkness—lack of vitamin D), high levels of stress, and culture shock.

What actions will you take today to guarantee you are around to enjoy the fruits of your labor with the people you have sacrificed so much for?

Below are some reality check questions for some groups in the U.S.

- Might you fare better in your home country?
- Might you have a higher level of well-being if you created a support system like the one back home?
- Will you come home to yourself today?

The truth is that we are of no use to anyone in a casket or living in an unhealthy state, whether physically, spiritually, mentally, or otherwise. You are worth the sleep and the quiet time to replenish without technology, social media, and the constant barrage of everyone's thoughts.

The Immigrants' Experience and Their Healthcare

In 2020, the overall life expectancy in the U.S. dropped by 1.5 years due to the COVID-19 pandemic. However, this reduction was not evenly distributed across the population. Native American individuals lost an average of four and a half years of life expectancy, Black and Hispanic individuals lost around three years, while White individuals lost only 1.2 years. These disparities align with broader health trends: Black and Hispanic people, as well as those living in poverty, experience worse health outcomes, including higher blood pressure, increased rates of diabetes, and maternal and infant mortality, compared to the overall population (Centers for Disease Control and Prevention (CDC).

Public health researcher Dr. Arline Geronimus from the University of Michigan challenges the traditional belief that these disparities are solely due to genetics, diet, and exercise. Instead, she introduces the concept of "weathering." Weathering refers to the chronic stress experienced by marginalized individuals due to poverty and discrimination. This ongoing stress damages their bodies at the cellular level, leading to increasingly severe health problems over time. Weathering accelerates the aging process, making individuals chronologically older than their actual age. In her book, *Weathering: The Extraordinary Stress of Ordinary Life in an Unjust Society*, Geronimus delves into this phenomenon. It is important to note that it is not a matter of every Black person having more damage than every White person; instead, it is about the cumulative impact of stress versus social context.

Understanding weathering illuminates the urgent need to address systemic injustice and create a more equitable society where health disparities are minimized and everyone can thrive.[xxvii]

(i) *On studying why Latin American immigrants, such as those from Mexico, have worsening health the longer they are in the U.S.* You are a fish out of water. If you have been raised in an immigrant family from Mexico, and then you are moving into predominantly White, American, affluent, and well-educated communities and institutions,... where you do not share the same assumptions or background, where the people you are working with do not appreciate all you have been through, where you are having to always be on your guard and manage how you portray yourself or present yourself to try and not fulfill stereotypes that you think people you are working with or going to school with might have about you....

That means you are at a certain level of vigilance and looking for cues everywhere about whether you belong, are welcome, and are subject to what many people call microaggressions. Those experiences themselves can cause weathering.

[Our health is] an indicator of…the context that we live in, of a society that is racist, oppressive, class conscious…. We will not solve health inequalities between Blacks and Whites or Latinx and Whites or other groups simply by getting people more education or higher incomes. If you stick with your group, this chronic stress arousal is more likely in unsupportive environments than…in more supportive environments. Weathering is not against social mobility; it is not for segregation or non-erasure. It is for seeing and recognizing what is happening and what it does to you biologically and realizing that if we want to eliminate health disparities or promote health equity, we must attend to what is happening in these different settings.

(ii) *On Improving the Maternal Mortality Rate*
Maternal mortality rates are on the rise, and it is becoming more evident that systemic racism within the healthcare system is a significant contributing factor. One way to address this issue is by having doulas or midwives attend births instead of physicians or by giving birth at home. These options can help reduce stress and ensure safety during childbirth. Unfortunately, there are not enough midwives, doulas, and maternity-care providers available, with only one provider per 15,000 births. Additionally, this number is not evenly distributed throughout the country. As a result, we need to train more people, such as OB-GYNs and midwives, to help address this issue.

In 2020, there were reports of verbal and physical abuse towards Asian and Black communities in public places. These communities were discriminated against solely because of their skin color and were even told to "go back to their country." Despite building a life in their immigrated countries through hard work, their identity was diminished to a mere "virus."

According to a report by Americanprogress.org, a policy to remove all undocumented immigrant workers from the workforce would cause a 2.6 percent reduction in the nation's GDP and a cumulative GDP reduction of $4.7 trillion over ten years. Even though immigrants make it appear easy, it is always considered their responsibility to adapt to people's different upbringings and navigate contradicting schools of thought and culture shocks with grace, often leaving them feeling isolated in a crowd. According to Teen Vogue, immigrant youth are more likely to be bullied than those born in the U.S.

A United Nations report on Violence against Children identifies refugees and children belonging to ethnic, racial, linguistic, cultural, or religious minorities as groups at higher risk of bullying. They point out that it may include bullying that targets another person's immigrant status or family history of immigration in the form of taunts, slurs, derogatory references to the immigration process, physical aggression, social manipulation, or exclusion because of their immigration status.[xxvi]

I have been privileged to enter the U.S. legally, be able to study, travel abroad, learn English (with an accent), and learn many other phenotypes, which may put me in a different box than many others. However, I have experienced many of the same issues Dr Geronimus has expressed above. I recall living in Philadelphia while pregnant and having to go to the hospital. I was automatically sent to the office that services Medicaid patients even though I had my private Blue Cross Blue Shield insurance. I later learned that another office usually services people with insurance, both connected to the Philadelphia hospital, but I was still sent to the Medicaid office. This is an example of unconscious bias in action: *I am Black, so I must be on Medicaid.*

My entire experience while I was at the hospital was shocking. Despite having health insurance, I saw firsthand how this office harmed their patients because they had Medicaid. Where does the *Do No Harm* in the Hippocratic Oath come into play? After having a few negative experiences, I requested my medical records and left for another hospital. This goes to show that even as an immigrant who arrived here legally, did my due diligence, acquired the necessary education, and earned a place as an employed person, I still had a turbulent experience giving birth to my first child. The recent ouster of the first Black female to be president of Harvard University and another Black female, a vice president (who died by suicide on 01/08/2024), goes to show that we are not protected from the vitriol that exists here in the U.S. It is often very challenging finding a Black doctor and many Black medical students detail stories of being forced out of medical programs or encouraged to study elsewhere.

The dynamic of unconscious and negative bias toward people of African descent in the U.S. is dire. It is a great concern to many who entered legally, came to add value, and sacrificed to make this country great. Still, they are often exposed to disparities and discrimination in health care and other public sectors.

The Immigrant Experience of Dating in America and the Modern Marriage

My journey towards meeting my husband was long, winding, full of obstacles, and sometimes confusing. The dating scene in the United States can be frustrating, heartbreaking, disorienting, and disappointing. In high school, I was used to receiving attention and compliments from male friends. When I started college, I received similar attention from several young men in the U.S. However, as I got older, I became increasingly disappointed with the options available. I often met young men who were content with being idle and not pursuing anything meaningful in their lives. On the other hand, I would also come across older men who claimed to be mature but had not even finished high school or earned a college degree. I would wonder what they had been doing with their lives all these years.

It was always confusing to me how some people could be born into a place full of opportunities but fail to recognize them. When I was still in college, a friend arranged for a young man to take me on a date. However, the experience was unpleasant as his car was filled with trash, and there was barely enough space to sit. When I refused to go on a second date, some of my friends criticized me for being too picky. I could not understand why they could not see that a person who does not put effort into making an excellent first impression is unlikely to change. Another friend wanted me to date her recently released brother from prison, but I ran for my life before being caught up in that entanglement. That is why I felt safer in church, as it provided me with guidelines to protect myself as a woman and avoid dangerous situations that could have derailed my career goals.

The other dynamic was coming across young men who expected you as a woman to chase them. I refused. This angered me. What kind of homes were these young men coming from? I am concerned about the pickings as my daughter matures in that season of her life. I see young women of all complexion dating, marrying, having children, and giving up their power to these men who cannot provide or do anything for them. I do understand that men give so much more than financial support, but how can one build a healthy family structure or home and provide for children if, at the very least, a man is not able to show that he can do that for himself or potentially do so for you and your children. The pressures were immense to stand against the dominant culture of settling around me and being criticized/pressured to get married as I got older.

Lesson: Ladies, please stop giving up your power by sleeping with men too early. Once you have bonded with a man emotionally, physically, and sexually, it is near impossible to walk away and keep your head clear.

Those around will hear me say: I completely understand why some cultures arrange marriages. It does take a village to choose a mate. Once your heart is invested in someone, you can no longer see clearly. Perhaps the best-case scenario could be a combination of family involved in the match and being chaperoned while getting to know each other.

I recently watched some period movies and marveled at how relationships were handled back then. I know we are in an age of women's liberation, but ladies, this often works against us. I see so many women broken from choosing poorly, being sexualized too early, or being test-driven by men in the dating phase.

Why would a man buy the cow if he already got the milk for free?

Observations have shown that men will not commit if you put the ball in their court as a woman. You do have power and a say in the matter. Do not fear using your brain—left-brain (masculine side). If you have no standards, you will accept anything. This is not about religious conservativism. Practically, this protects your honor and future as a woman. Let us be smart with how we protect ourselves and stop giving our power to men and others when it comes to dating, courting, and selecting a partner for marriage. You have both feminine and masculine within you. Use both to your advantage.

Marriage in America can be challenging due to social pressures and unrealistic expectations. Many couples feel they must compete with others by showing off their latest luxury possessions, which often leads to financial instability. However, my husband and I have decided to prioritize healthy financial decisions and not worry about impressing others. We have noticed that many couples struggle to make wise financial choices due to social pressures, and it takes time to build wealth. My husband and I are careful who we hang around with because, inevitably, the mindset we are looking for is often missing—the constant comparison and judgment. We have sought to make healthy financial decisions and could care less about impressing any Joneses. Still, it is interesting how many couples buckle under pressure to buy expensive cars, homes, and name-brand clothing they cannot afford. We know several folks who have had to turn in cars and other items because their budgets would not allow it.

We have observed just how challenging it is for new couples to focus on making healthy financial and other choices because of social pressures surrounding them in this country. It takes years for a family to build wealth. It is not done overnight. Please do not compare yourself with someone else who appears publicly to be further ahead of you. I would like to see the financials of some of these couples donning luxury cars and expensive homes and wonder how much pressure their families live under when they are behind closed doors. Take a look at the statistics of the saving rate of everyday Americans. I know firsthand because we worked for a year and a half with a financial coach at the start of our marriage and heard stories of what he observed (not names or anything, but broadly shared of what he saw with extravagant spending, lack of savings, and financial discipline).

We are all on our journeys. The constant comparison benefits none of us. We have decided to integrate the healthy aspects of the immigrant financial mentality with research-based recommendations on being frugal with our hard-earned income. Whenever we return to the island, I have noted examples of couples and feel the difference in the air around us. The priority is a healthy family union, not impressing others. Here, it is like an unseen element driving you apart. The unrealistic expectations and standards are too top-heavy. So, we monitor what comes in and influences our decision to stay married and from whom we take marriage advice. It is indeed a battle when you walk into that marriage ring because, in this culture, it seems a fashionable fad to have a marriage unraveling at the seams.

It is worth noting that the kind of support that one would receive in a small, close-knit community is often absent in the United States. Here are some of the factors to consider:

> **Communal Support:** There is a sense of shared responsibility in tight-knit communities such as those in our home countries. Experienced couples offer guidance, wisdom, and emotional support to younger ones. This communal safety net helps to strengthen relationships.

> **U.S. Individualism:** The United States is an individualistic society that emphasizes personal responsibility. While this independence has its benefits, it can also lead to isolation. Marriage ministries often focus on ceremonies rather than ongoing support.

> **Building Your Community:** Having a support network is crucial for a married couple. Seek out like-minded friends, attend workshops, and invest in your relationship. Don't rely solely on external structures; actively nurture your marriage.

> **Proactivity and Intentionality:** It is important to be proactive and intentional. Seek knowledge, attend counseling, and prioritize your relationship. Remember that a healthy marriage requires effort and continuous learning.

Cultural Context: Recognize that cultural context shapes expectations. While the U.S. lacks communal structures, you can still find pockets of support—whether through friends, mentors, or online communities.

In this "other world," navigating requires resilience, adaptability, and a commitment to building a thriving marriage.

How does one choose a mate in this confusing culture? Have you pondered as I did? I have observed and felt the pressure to choose a mate based solely on physical appearance, only to realize later that I had selected a monster. The person you marry is not the physical structure but the personality and spirit that occupies that physical body. You see it when someone dies; the body remains, and the actual personality and spirit are no longer there. Be sure to lift the hood and try to discern the real issues you will face after the fancy, expensive wedding. Look for evidence of the fundamental problems in your spouse and their family as the festivities settle and the real personality emerges. People spend so much on weddings but struggle to make ends meet after the big wedding event.

There are things about the American culture which continue to baffle, amaze, and concern many immigrants. The culture appears to be moving towards and farther away from what many would call common sense or, to some, as conservative. For example, women want to replace men in the work world. The desire to wear less clothing or to be the opposite of modest or proper. This looks like a rebellion against common sense social norms to new immigrants. Perhaps some have been raised in very strict or conservative environments and wish to swing to the other side of that mindset. This desire to be different from conservatives may lead many to go too far to the left or wherever these behaviors end up.

I was never one to follow groups. From a young girl, I had very firm sentiments about how I wanted to interact socially or otherwise. Perhaps that is why I never fit in with many groups. The choice and pickings appeared slim regarding common sense or safe behavior. The past Christmas 2023, I went to Walmart for mixed fruits as I had found it there previously in preparation for baking the traditional Jamaican fruit cake (also known in the U.S. as black cake—I guess to differentiate from other types of fruit cakes in the U.S.). With difficulty finding the product, I stopped an employee and asked if she could direct me to find the product. Her first response left me in shock. "I do not cook," she said with a grin. She explained that she did not know what I was looking for and sent me to the bakery to inquire. The initial feeling stayed with me for weeks. I pondered how we (the U.S. culture) got to this place.

When did all these nurturing qualities become such a rarity and culturally unacceptable? Cooking for my family and friends is a beautiful and fulfilling feeling. Our family's women (and men) have a tradition of nurturing through cooking. Traditional nurturing activities are now being frowned upon, and adopting traditionally masculine behaviors is becoming more acceptable. In a loud culture where common sense does not appear to be common, in our home, our daughter will learn how to cook and have the option to study to her heart's content. I have heard stories of women expressing that they wished they thought of having children and starting a family at a certain age. My hope for the next generation of females in our family is that they take a commonsense position when balancing the desire for educational aspirations and motherhood. I have achieved many things, but nothing fills me like being a mother and nurturing our family through cooking, caring for our homes, and operating from my feminine energy.

The Immigrant Experience with Healthcare

Can you imagine living in a country and being unsure whether when you go to the doctor to seek medical attention, you will be getting the best care or whether you will be abused or have something done to erase you? Lately, I have pondered a story I heard on National Public Radio (NPR) about African Americans sharing a book of safe places they could stop for shelter, food, or assistance post-slavery, Jim Crow, the Civil Rights movement, reconstruction, and so on, whether immigrants needed the same. I have found myself asking for referrals before just showing up at any doctor's office because of the uncertainty that I may be met with hostility, poor treatment, or something else despite having great insurance. These folks might as well put a sign up that read, "No BIPOCs Allowed." At a recent dental visit, my dentist of four years suggested that I seek a specialist for a procedure. I explained that unless she had a referral, I would not be inclined to choose from a list around town because I did not feel safe doing so, and that is an example of what it means to be Black in America. How did this country get here? After two decades in the U.S., the feelings of being unsafe as a Black woman have never been more present. In fact, as an immigrant, I cannot remember feeling so unsafe. Is this a healthy country for me to raise our daughter, for people with accents, for people who look like me?

These questions and sentiments led me to start my podcast, *The Immigrant Experience in America.* I needed to talk about it and hear other experiences and perspectives.

Mom was diagnosed with (breast cancer) after arriving in the U.S. No one around us had ever discussed the healthcare system in the U.S. before moving here, so we had a general assumption that healthcare in the U.S. was of high quality and some of the best in the world. Mom had given up a business to be in the U.S. and was now starting over in a new country. She had worked for 10+ years and paid social security, and all other required taxes directly from her salary biweekly.

Our family struggled to provide Mom with the best care possible. She was blessed to have encountered some excellent doctors who demonstrated they were doing their best for her. But, in the in-between, we would encounter so many hurdles trying to get her access to support, which was available to survivors of breast cancer and current patients. We had one attendant asking which country she was from on several occasions. I was not always present, as work had me traveling or living internationally on several occasions. We tried over several years of re-application, and this lady kept asserting that Mom was born somewhere else even though she had a U.S. passport and had naturalized many years previously. This angered me and exhausted me. Toward the end of Mom's life, we had a doctor recommend that we stop checking her blood pressure at the request of a prescription to get a digital machine to monitor her blood pressure so we would not have to prick her so often. This resulted in Mom's condition worsening and being unable to walk as we missed the moment her blood pressure plummeted. We have since discussed and pondered whether it was this doctor's negligence that caused our mom to lose the battle with breast cancer.

At one point, I sought out legal guidance to see whether we had a case against this organization and its employees. Racism, prejudice, ignorance, anti-immigrant sentiments at its best. It was as if we were outside, whatever resources were available at our fingertips, and we could not get past the gatekeeper. I was angry. I have been paying taxes, and so had Mom for years, and now that we needed the support to buffer what we could already do for ourselves, we faced hurdles. I could not understand how illegal immigrants were getting access to medical resources. Still, my mom, who entered legally and was a U.S. citizen, had to fight to access a system to which she had already contributed. I often wondered whether this idea of "weathering" and stress was part of what caused my mom's health to fail. She had a green thumb and made healthy meals but worked nights for several years and could not fully rest during the day.

Before migrating, be sure to ask questions of people already living here before leaving an emotionally safe environment where you can trust the medical care you receive. Access to proper healthcare is precarious at best for Blacks and other immigrants.

You may find yourself on an erasure list being served by someone with an agenda of which you may be ignorant, as is the case for many immigrants.

In 2018, I had my first experience with a doula,[3] but unfortunately, it was not a good one. I had moved to Philadelphia for a job opportunity and was pregnant with my first child. Being away from my family, I wanted to hire a doula for support during the labor process. I found a White female from New York with an impressive resume online and hired her. While she brought some materials and showed up for initial meetings, she proved incompetent in the end. A month or two before my due date, she told me she would not be available on my delivery day and attempted to forward me to her friend. However, I missed connecting with her friend as I was working and unable to take calls most of the day. As my due date neared, I contacted her for guidance, but she sent me to the hospital instead of coming to my home, which is what a doula is supposed to do.

By the time I reached the hospital, I was already in labor and had to make do with my prepared bag and a list of instructions for the nurse. She arrived at the hospital the next day after I had spent a painful night. I had to take an epidural as the pain was too unbearable, and everything I had prepared for went out the window. The nurse found her annoying and asked where I had found her. I could not believe it when she dared to ask my cousin to bring her something to eat while I was in labor. She even mentioned that she had to return home because her husband had toothache issues. Later, when she returned, she walked through the door as my baby was being born. I was shocked that I had paid her in full for no service at all.

Unfortunately, this country has many frauds, and thorough research is essential before hiring someone for such an important role.

Maneuvering the American Workplace

I learned the idea of self-interest for the first time while an undergrad. It took me the longest time to understand, even though I knew the words. Working in America was a disorientating experience for me. I was a highly motivated young woman who knew nothing more than to do her best. I had the best and worst days at these companies: Kmart, Firstar Bank, Country Club Bank, State Street Bank, and public sector roles. My biggest issue was feeling like no one would look out for me or provide mentorship. I felt lost in many spaces and lacked a sense of belonging, meaning, or connectedness. In the early years of my career, I had no understanding of the systems I was dealing with nor language to explain my experiences. Microaggression,

---

3 A woman employed to provide guidance and support to the mother of a newborn baby.

discrimination, salary negotiation, employee resource groups, the intersection of being a woman + immigrant + woman of color, and the challenges that came along with these labels were foreign to me—a dangerous combination of ignorance and nakedness. Our family was new to the U.S., and we were all simultaneously figuring out the culture and work world.

Labor has always been a huge issue in the United States. Capitalism demands it: first slavery, then indentured labor, then skilled and unskilled immigration to feed the beast. The U.S. is the only place I have worked, so my experience is limited to this context.

It can feel like social media is everywhere these days. Recently, I came across a young lady sharing a situation where she was in a training program with several other females, one of whom was a Black female. She went on to say that the Black female was very skilled in her teaching approach. She could not find anything to criticize, BUT she felt some way about the Black female being the best in the program of all the other females. As I watched this, I had a light bulb moment and immediately responded, "Oh, that was what I experienced." For years, I could not find the language to explain why I would go from the office pet to the office threat. I would be hired to do a job, I felt I aced the interview and felt competent, but I would start feeling like others around me were treating me differently. I experienced this in all-White office spaces where I was the only Black female, in mixed office environments with a little of everyone, and in all-Black workspaces. The experience that flashed before my eyes as I watched the above TikTok video was in late 2017 when I attended a work training program. I was voted the winner of three other employees who vied to be the class leader. It felt great to attend meetings and report back to the class. I was more observant in the meeting and taking notes back to the class. However, towards the end of the class, I had what I would call a groundbreaking proposal for the Program Manager to get more enthusiasm towards class participation. She documented it and praised my suggestion. Would you believe that the other leaders in the class who had dominated the conversation in previous weeks became hostile and resorted to ostracizing me for the remainder of the training program? I was shocked and felt quite hurt. They stopped speaking or responding to my greetings. What? What did I do? I felt so confused. Anyway, I completed my responsibilities and continued with my life, but the experience never left me. This TikToker, in one video, explained exactly what happened. There seems to be such an aversion towards Black leadership in this country, and it took me years to decode it after ample experiences of being passed over for promotion and others trying to sabotage my career. While in college and working my darnedest to do well, I had never pondered the idea that I would get to the point where people would deny me the merit I deserved. However, this is a reality for so many Black females. They say that Blacks have to be more than 2x better.

I often feel that immigrants are held to impossibly high standards—expected to be perfect or even multiple times better than their peers. It can be disheartening to receive backhanded compliments as if our achievements are somehow unearned. I am sure there will be evidential case studies on both sides, but I know these realizations are now at the top of my mind everywhere I go. I am even more vigilant about which business places I enter without a referral. I am more vigilant about who I interact with and wonder if they are safe. I find that I am sensitive about things that would previously have rolled off my shoulder/back. As Kaara Kidjoe expressed, we enter this country with openness and innocence to be friendly and kind to all people of all colors. Now, we are forced to grapple with a system created by one group of people and perpetrated by many who stand to benefit from it. I still take the position that those of us immigrants who were raised outside of this racialized environment were privileged to have had those experiences. Our thoughts have energy. Now that these thoughts are constantly in my psyche, I find they impact the energy I bring daily. I have been very intentional about meditative practices to rid myself of the realities around me. One, I will endeavor not to allow toxic people to rent space in my mind for free. I was born with the same freedoms as all other humans and was not raised to be a second-class citizen. How long and far will you choose to raise your children comfortably but ill-prepare them for the real world or life in general? Philosophers will tell you that greatness comes with effort, but why do some people believe they must be handed things without earning them? This is an example of the American work world. You can have the same credentials and not be given the space to contribute authentically because others fear your light and smarts. They expect you to dim your light so their bleak light can shine. They want you to put in the work while they take the credit.

CHAPTER 6

*Without clarity and purpose, you cannot
distinguish an opportunity from a distraction.*
—Gary Henderson / unknown.

Surrender to your Life's Purpose and Let Go of People-Pleasing

The U.S. is where many can finally ponder any idea of self and how that relates to the collective. The U.S. creates a safe space for many to free themselves from the unhealthy entanglements of many collective cultures. Colonialism and religion taught people to be humble and not to talk about themselves. In contrast, collectivist cultures teach that the collective is more important than the individual.

Loneliness and isolation are two main downsides to living long-term in this U.S. culture. You may be isolated from loved ones for many reasons. For example, globalization now forces many of us to travel and live wherever employment takes us. On the other hand, it could be by choice as many people opt to "get their own place" because we are now in an environment that supports that financially, and so many of us end up lonely and isolated from the communal settings in which we were initially raised. Many of us from communal settings do not realize this until we are in a position where we must face ourselves, so we run back to the external validation of our families of origin or communities of origin, be they dysfunctional or unhealthy. However, why are we so afraid of facing ourselves?

If you do not love yourself, you need people to love you. This is a sad state, as you are left to the ups and downs of people's personalities because you are uncomfortable with the person you see inside. This could be because we were taught that we are sinful and have a terrible nature, or we are oblivious to how our actions and search for acceptance drive us to please. You can only love others to the degree you love yourself.

Self-love is a result of self-discovery.

Self-love is a result of knowing your source.

Self-love is a result of self-worth and recognizing your self-worth.

It can be a crazy thing to realize that you are not loving yourself. Have you ever come to this realization? This culture leads us to buy things because people equate collecting things to having self-value. This is capitalism at its best to keep you as a consumer and not realize that you do not need a Nike tennis shoe or Louis Vuitton purse to have value. You arrived with self-love as a baby, and it never left and cannot be destroyed or harmed. The Bible says: "Neither life nor death can separate you from the love of God." Self-love is a result of self-esteem.

Esteem = true value/worth. Are you keeping people around you because you feel seen by their presence? Have you ever considered going on a "come home to yourself" journey so you can see your true value?

Self-love = self-concept (picture). The picture we hold of ourselves should never come from other people. Do not allow people to paint you or tell you who you are. Avoid living for compliments from others to determine how you feel about yourself. For many, acceptance and the idea of self are foreign ideas from a collectivist culture where the focus has always been on group cohesion and pleasing others. The journey to self-discovery/discovering you can be a painful but liberating process.

People's perception of you impacts how you see yourself because you depend on external validation. Self-love is a result of identity. How much do you value yourself? Discovering your identity determines how much you love yourself and how you interact with others.

Self-love = self-confidence.

Self-love = self-motivation.

Self is manifested in self-values. A person who loves themselves or values who they are builds people up to where they are and not vice versa, but on the opposite perspective, it also means that you are so healed and whole that you can sit with and give of yourself no matter the circumstance or situation.

Self-love provides you with the equipment to give to someone of yourself with no attachment.

Self-love is self-forgiving. Forgiving yourself first before expecting others to forgive you.

Self-love is manifested in self-investment. We were created to influence the world around us. The key to influence is value: if you want success, seek to influence, create an impact, and not chase being successful. The influencer attracts success. Value is determined by the work you bring to life.

You were created to dominate life
but in an area of gifting/purpose —Miles Munroe

I struggled more in some workplaces than others, especially as I worked overseas in certain capacities. It felt like I was having an out-of-body experience every day at work. I wanted to run from the people I saw around me; the egos were often too much to deal with. I could not envision myself becoming what I saw exhibited around me. The kind of leadership that leaves you confused with your jaw on the ground, asking how this incompetent person got this job or position. Self-discovery, development, refinement, and serving it to the world will result in significance *(Miles Monroe, "Keys to Self-Love," YouTube)*. Your gift attracts wealth and affluence. People are attracted to your gift; they are not attracted to you, per se.

A man's gift makes room for him,
And brings him before great men.—Proverbs 18:16-17

Your gift will make room for you; it opens doors. Your gift makes you more attractive than your looks. Affluence means being rich in personal motivation, significance (important to life), a sense of destiny, generational responsibility, material comfort, and being in charge of one's life. Be fruitful—bring forth what is on the inside.

What is your primary passion?

How do you release your seed?

Your seed attracts your wealth and keeps you free from economic crisis. When you refine your seed, it protects you from the economy. This teaching by Miles Munroe confirms how important it is to come home to yourself. Stop giving up your power to other people by seeking their validation. There is definitely a place for mentorship, coaching, and consultation. However, the way it is often practiced in U.S. culture can lead people to prioritize external success and attention over their well-being. This can result in a sense of emptiness, even after achieving success, and a need to focus on personal growth and self-awareness.

Are you a high achiever? A high-achieving immigrant woman, a man who has steamed ahead and did what your parents expected of you by excelling educationally, socially, and otherwise. You were the golden child. You received the baton, and you completed your leg of the race. Only you are sad inside and feeling disconnected from it all. Unable to enjoy the fruits of your labor because you are still striving for more. Your mind has been conditioned to solve problems, fix things needing fixing, give of yourself where support is required, and sacrifice to help others climb, find themselves, or have bread to eat or a roof over your head. You have achieved the proverbial "have it all," but you are numb.

Life seems to have you on a train from one thing to the next, and things appear automated. Wait, do you have a say in all this? You are missing out on the joys of ordinary life. People in your life seem to be enjoying your presence or what you have provided, but you cannot seem to slow down to experience it or feel the happiness, joy, and peace that is already around you, so you continue to strive for the next thing because you are in pursuit of happiness. Perhaps the next thing will bring you that joy you seek so desperately. That peace you are hoping will arrive at the next accomplishment. That connectedness to the many people always buzzing around you. You feel empty despite all the knowledge acquisition, accolades, professional connections, degrees on the wall, the spouse, the beautiful home, the cars, the children, vacations, and all you have ever wanted. It is here, but you are somewhere else looking for the next achievement, goal, or thing to conquer. You ask yourself, does life ever slow down? Is this it? Where is the happiness or joy that I thought would come when I finally achieved the things on my list? You look back and see all the days you have rushed through, missed because you were never present; your mind was looking to the next feat to conquer, the next high to impress your family/ community/colleagues, but the highs only last for a brief moment. Hence, you are on to your next fix - chasing after the thing that will fill you up, fill you with joy and happiness, the thing that will satisfy your soul, the thing that will cause you to give up the chase, but it never works.

I think of Anthony Bourdain, Kate Spade, Robin Williams, and Twitch, people who would be considered highly successful but shocked us with how their lives ended. Success after success, achievement after achievement, degree after degree, drink after drink, sex partner after sex partner, daring challenge after daring challenge—anything to help you feel alive, to connect to something, to finally find meaning and purpose, to finally find significance. You are disappointed every time you achieve the next feat. This was me after years of achieving, conquering, stretching myself, seeking to please, making others proud, sacrificing to pull up others while climbing, fixing problems, catching balls I should have allowed to drop, and giving support to people who did not appreciate it. I wanted more for others than they wanted for themselves, and so on. It was a never-ending cycle of neglecting Simone, of rescuing everyone else while they could not rescue me when I needed it the most. I was exhausted, disconnected, empty, sad, unmotivated, and burnt out. *I had become a 'human-doing,' a machine-like entity ideal for a capitalistic economy.*

It was January 1, 2023, two years exactly after my mom's passing, which rocked my world and shifted everything. All I could think about was doing what I was meant to do on this earth. I was getting healthy so I could be here as long as I could for our daughter, as I felt I had buried my mom way too early. How could I get to that aliveness and purposeful living I had sought all these years? It seems so fleeting every time I conquer an achievement, and it would only last for a moment. I was numb, depressed, filled with anxiety, and constantly busied myself. I would sit with our daughter, and my mind would be off daydreaming about the next thing I needed to do, achieve, a place to be, a never-ending cycle of comparing myself to people around me. When does it end? Will I ever be satisfied? What will it take to give up the crazy chase of pleasing others and searching for external validation?

I decided to do an experiment. I will practice saying no to everyone and everything as much as possible, to go on a journey to find those things that could bring me simple joys. I was missing out on all my achievements, family, child, and the fullness of my life because I was always living in the past or the future and never the present. This is the year I came home to myself. Emptiness forced me to slow down, choose deliberately, go into nature, say no, meditate, and journal about the simple joys already existing in my present life to make space for Simone's joy to emerge. This had to be Simone's time. I had spent the last 20+ years pleasing everyone else but myself, rescuing one person after another, fixing problems. I was missing all the blessings already in my life and constantly seeking the next thing I thought would finally make me happy. That was enough of a wake-up call—a call to come home to myself.

You always say yes and don't know how to say no.
If you don't know how to say no, you spend time doing things
you don't want to do. You can't organize your day, and you can't
do your day as you wish because you are at the disposal
of other people. You never please yourself and constantly
please everyone else. I am 50 years old, and now
I have learned how to say no.—Actress, Sophia Loren

The Year I Surrendered to My Purpose

My life, as I am aware of it, has been a rush, pushing myself, saying yes, giving financially or otherwise, afraid to say no, no matter how sick or depleted I was to succeed or show up for people. The passing of my mom on January 1, 2021, served as a jarring wake-up call, making me realize that I was no longer a child. I vividly remember spending Christmas Day, 12/25/2020, amid the height of the pandemic, on the phone with doctors and seeking advice from our family members in the medical field on how to navigate some end-of-life decisions. It was a heavy burden to bear at a young age. Mom was only 69 years old but had been battling breast cancer for more than ten years. The doctors had told my sister and me the day before that Mom was in the final stages and that they would need to intubate her (put a tube down her throat) to feed her and warn of the possibility that she might choke. I was livid. She had put her hands in our mouth and indicated that she was hungry while we visited her. It was during COVID-19, and we were only allowed to visit her at the hospital on a limited basis. She had not eaten in days since her blood sugar dropped precipitously, and she fell while getting up to walk. How did she deteriorate so quickly? Only a week before, she had shown signs of improving while a family member visited. One primary care physician told my sister to stop checking my mom's blood sugar levels as we asked for a prescription to get a different type of device to monitor her blood sugar as we had to prick her fingers, causing her to bleed numerous times during the day. Within the space of one week, she went from lucid and talking to being unable to stand on her own and in the emergency room not being able to eat. Can you imagine our confusion and numbness? To be faced with doctors advising against giving your mother food and insisting that she would choke. It did not make any sense. She asked for food, and we could only feed her with a spoon and liquids.

Something changes when a parent passes away. The veil is lifted, and the realization dawns that they are no longer in this dimension. While grieving and helping my sister make burial arrangements for our mother (from abroad), the gravity of the situation hit me. I realized that we were planning our mom's funeral. It was a sobering moment that made me think about my health and the need to take care of myself for the sake of my two-and-a-half-year-old daughter and future generations. I returned to work feeling numb and dizzy at times. I remember sitting in my office staring out the window at the sky, wondering where our mom's spirit was now. Was she sitting in my office or floating in the clouds, watching us? I am not sure how we made it through those months. The funeral home was a hot mess. They lied about when the death certificate was signed and held Mom's body for an entire month so they could make more money. This is where one can see the lowest points of humanity—trying to profit off someone's death. If you ever have to do an international funeral—shipping a body—make sure to get recommendations and do thorough research, as most funeral homes in the U.S. are not helpful and are uneducated about the process of shipping a body for burial internationally.

There was something about Mom's passing that lit a fire in my belly to do anything I needed to do right away. She passed 18 days shy of her 70th birthday. I started realizing months later just how depleted I was feeling. I was exhausted with little energy to cook, care for my child, and maintain work responsibilities. It was just too much. I was psychologically drained! Worrying about who needed help while I was bleeding. This is what codependency and lack of boundaries, very prevalent in people from collectivist cultures, will drive you to do. I often could not sleep trying to figure out how to help someone accomplish some project with which they had requested assistance. Wishing to work from home, I accepted a job towards the end of the COVID-19 pandemic, which later required me to move and travel frequently out of State. This only added to my stress, exhaustion, and psychological strain.

At the end of each year, I typically take some time to reflect and choose a word or energy that I want to embody for the upcoming year. However, after listening to various podcasts, talks, and audiobooks, I realized that I had been neglecting myself. I noticed a significant lack of energy, self-control, and overwhelming emotions. It became clear that I couldn't continue living my daily life as it was. I finally admitted to myself that I didn't know how to say no, and saying yes to everything was driving me crazy.

My word for 2023 was SURRENDER. Surrender to God's plan for me. It was certainly not his purpose or design for me to run myself to the ground like this. I was depressed and thought leaving my marriage and child would somehow bring me peace. You know something is broken, not right, or seriously out of alignment when you are daydreaming about a documentary you watched where a mom left her husband and children to move to the other side of the country and that she was a better mom by meeting with her children virtually. This was the breaking point. There began my journey home to myself!

CHAPTER 7

*The essence of being human
is that one does not seek perfection.*
—George Orwell

Have You Become a 'Human-doing'?

Recently, I met up with a friend, and as she detailed some recent events in her life, I could feel the passion and tears welling up inside me. She is a high-achieving immigrant woman just like me, and after years of taking care of everything, she is now realizing some of the patterns that do not serve her. After commiserating with her, I began to ask myself:

How did we get here?

How did we become this person who completes task after task and is unsure how to slow down, care for myself, or feel joy?

Meet Denise. She described how she left her job to start her own business, but her employer did not react well. She mentioned how she returned to the store to support her former employer by making a purchase, but they were rude to her. They refused to give her an employee discount, which she had to complain about. When I asked her why she even returned to support them, she explained that they were struggling to meet their sales targets. She realized that she and many people she knows have a pattern of being overly accommodating, often described as "too nice." Later, her therapist also advised her that she was too agreeable.

I once stumbled upon a book titled *No More Nice Christian Girl.* The book discusses how girls and women are taught to be nice right from birth. This message is so deeply ingrained in our subconscious that we tend to respond nicely, even when it is not in our best interest, and could result in harm. This is particularly true for high-achieving immigrant women like my friend.

Our conversation continued as we discussed why she does so much and how she can try to become a stronger person. I advised: "It is not about being tougher but caring more for yourself and saying no more often." She agreed, and we talked about how she identified as an alpha female—which she really was not, as she has never stood up for herself.

I have been compared to an alpha female—assertive, confident, and highly motivated. However, I initially did not possess these qualities when I arrived in the United States. Well, I was confident and highly motivated but had to work hard on the becoming assertive part. I believe the culture of striving and achievement here has developed such a personality. Over the years, life circumstances and experiences have molded me into who I am today. I recall feeling responsible for setting an example for many over the years. I was motivated to make my family proud and look good. After years of adjusting to this capitalistic, industrial culture, I became a 'human-doing.' Upon moving here, I lost touch with my sense of being and connection to others. I began to question the person I was becoming. I had become a taskmaster in my daily life, at work, home, and even in my interactions with others.

What happened to me?

It occurred to me that the end goal, finishing the task, and getting to the expected result over everything else was paramount to me. I did not like the person I had transformed into after years of giving up who I was at the core. At my core, I felt more connected organically to life, the people around me, and the belonging associated with being raised in a small farm town of less than 250 people. The slightest deviation from the goal would trigger me, and I would become a person I no longer recognize or like.

Finding Meaning

I had the marriage, the child I prayed for, the home, the job, and many other blessings, but I was still a 'human doing.' I had not slowed down. Every time I achieved something, I would move the target because the satisfaction of that achievement was only momentary.

What is the matter with me?

I had a wonderful husband, a bright, beautiful, intuitive child, and a comfortable home, yet I was chasing something else to fill me. That is the reality of life in the U.S. A little competition is healthy. On one hand, it is one of the things that set the U.S. economic model of constant innovation and production, but it can drive people to this constant striving, insatiable appetite to achieve and people-please. It becomes particularly problematic for people from collectivist cultures who are taught no boundaries and to please people from birth. In this season, I slowed to see that this was never going to fill my soul and decided to stop chasing happiness but rather meaning and joy.

You are the love of your life! When you start with yourself, loving yourself, creating boundaries, advocating for yourself, and being honest with yourself and not being so good that you're not being honest. Everything grows from there. It is the greatest seed you can plant in the world. To create great friendships and relationships is to love yourself. —Actress, Viola Davis

Culture and the Science of the Brain and Mind

In collectivist cultures, girls would likely take on typical feminine roles and boys the atypical masculine roles. Of course, this is not the same across the board, as gender dynamics likely differ from country to country and culture to culture in how girls and boys are raised in collectivist cultures. Dealing with people in individualistic cultures and how it can leave us feeling like our kindness is not being reciprocated. People are in it for themselves. They take what they want or need and leave with no feelings about it. The opposite is also dangerous, where men and women from collectivist cultures can become so stretched and scattered in focusing on everyone else but their families. Children and spouses suffer from this family setting because there are no healthy boundaries to meet the family's needs, marriage, and children before offering oneself, time, and resources to others outside that unit. This breaks up many marriages and causes strain on relationships. As high-achieving immigrant women, it can become especially problematic to find a spousal match that allows you to operate from your feminine energy simply because you have likely studied, can provide financially, and do many masculine tasks. However, looking for balance with whomever you choose to marry is vital.

Operating from my feminine energy is vital to maintaining balance in my life. However, cultural differences can create friction, especially when choosing a partner from an individualistic culture versus someone from a collectivist background. In an individualistic culture, personal independence is often prioritized, while family and community ties play a central role in a collectivist culture. This can lead to different expectations and challenges in a relationship. It's important to seek a partner who understands the need for healthy and flexible boundaries with their family of origin or former culture. This ensures that both partners can honor their backgrounds while creating a harmonious and balanced relationship.

Jack moved to the U.S. after living decades in a collectivist setting with his family of origin. While excited to join his spouse in a new country, Jack felt the palpable conflict of feeling like he was abandoning his family of origin as his parents saw him as their right-hand person. Jack later struggled to adapt to the individualistic culture of having a nuclear family of his own and implementing healthy boundaries with his family of origin. There were instances where Jack felt the pull to be present and available and needed to prioritize his nuclear family, but that clashed with feelings of guilt, shame, and pleasing many in his former culture and life. Jack particularly struggles with maintaining healthy boundaries with his parents and siblings as he was raised in an enmeshed type of family setting. The word boundary was non-existent in Jack's mind and in his former culture. They shared everything, including intimate details about marriage, spousal relationships, finances in his nuclear family, continuation of religious participation, and other expectations from his family of origin. Jack's family of origin struggled to set him free to fully experience and manage his new nuclear family. In fact, old responsibilities from his family of origin, religious community, and social relationships continued for years into his marriage as Jack struggled with saying no and people-pleasing. This eventually led to enormous strains on Jack's marriage and relationship with his spouse to the point of divorce."

Lesson: If you're from a collectivist culture, be sure to watch out for the narcissistic, 'what is in it for me people' in this culture. From birth, they have been taught to only think of themselves and often are incapable of caring for others unless they are getting something out of it. Many people from this individualistic culture must be taught to think of others more and less of themselves. It is all about a certain balance. Neither extreme benefits anyone. Immigrants from collectivist cultures are not like that.

We give with no strings attached.

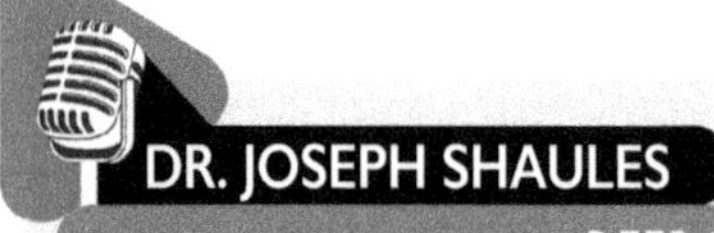

EPISODES 18

Finding meaning is more important than finding happiness. People like to feel good, so we associate happiness with positive emotions. Research into resilience, which is the ability to deal with adversity, finds that if you chase happiness, you end up less happy. [On the other hand] if you chase meaning, you end up with more life satisfaction.

Often, though, we end up empty if we are not careful to be selective with the people in our inner circle. We need givers in our inner circle just as much as we are givers. It has taken years for me to slow down to see that I have been attracting people who take and leave. My well was always drying up. You will have to inventory your life and possibly let go of relationships that do not support you. Everyone has their own guidance system and responsibility for their own life. We need to allow people to experience the consequences of their actions so they grow and change just like we have had to do.

Rescuing people from their actions does not allow them to mature and change. If we are to focus on our own lives and responsibilities, we find there is not much energy to be running other people's lives for them. You would be surprised to see what people are capable of if we stop the roles we play and allow space for them to catch their own balls. If we catch people's balls, we inevitably neglect our own balls. Drop those balls. Stop catching those balls. Allow people to catch their balls.

Please repeat after me this affirmation:
I release others to experience the life that is meaningful to them,
and I release myself to create the life that is meaningful to me.
We are all guided by divine wisdom
—Louise Hay

We have to learn to love ourselves

We cannot love others until we love ourselves. That is codependency and neediness. No one can love you enough if you do not already love yourself. You have to be complete and whole to love and give from a healthy place, but on the other hand, watch out for empty people who will mask themselves to be around you, in your presence, so that they can fill their love tank from your well. These people will take from your well until they get what they want and disappear. This is essential when dating men in this country and finding a life partner. Often, they are incapable of thinking of anyone's needs except their own. They aim to test drive until they get what they want and have no regrets about using women, and the same occurs with women who do the same to men as well. Trust your inner wisdom and go within to guide you alongside your inner circle (there to help you see past your blind spots). We have been talked out of following our own guidance system and intuition by the church, parents, family, friends, capitalism, and other culprits. You do know what to do if you slow down to listen. Stop giving up your power to others. Use your God-given connection with your inner self (some call it the God connection) and spiritual self to guide your life. If you practice, you will see that the inner voice is always there, guiding you, and it will, over time, become louder and clearer. Just slow down and stop letting people talk you out of what you already know to be true. Learn to go within to hear your inner wisdom. The answers are all within you. Sometimes it is outside as well. God will confirm or show you signs in the world, but you must slow down and be in tune to hear and see the messages. Positive affirmations create a positive life. As we create safety and security in our minds, we will see and find it in the world we experience. Your mind is powerful.

Finding your voice

The journey to finding my voice has been a challenging one—as I try to return to who I was upon arrival. It is wise to observe more than be too chatty, as this culture would try to convince us that this is the way to be. My personality was one of being more observant when I first moved to the U.S., and then I got bamboozled into racing to be the first to speak and appear smart. Sometimes, being younger in collectivist cultures can be difficult, as those considered senior in age can use their position to manipulate and train you to play roles that serve them.

Finding one's voice in collectivist and individualistic settings can be difficult. As a young adult, I remember not knowing what I thought about things because, many times, there was no space for me to express myself. I had to go on a journey of quieting the voices, thoughts, and perspectives of others to find my own. I had to come home to myself.

Burnout

Burnout: I have come to realize that I have been suffering from burnout for several years. It ebbs and flows and is more intense at different periods/seasons. Looking back, it appeared more prevalent while I worked at a federal job. I have moved approximately 20 times over the last 24 years. I have been on flights to another city or country approximately 50+ times. I have lived, worked, or temporarily visited Africa (Sierra Leone, Ghana), Europe (France, UK), Latin America (Mexico), the Caribbean (Dominican Republic (DR), Cuba, Guantanamo Bay, Jamaica), and Canada. For this reason, I ended up with a job that required me to travel monthly for program management (Guantanamo et al. (GTMO), Accra - Police Training, Mexico - Consular Affairs - visiting incarcerated U.S. citizens), plus trying to make family events back in the U.S. while I was living and working abroad.

What is burnout? According to *Psychology Today*, "Burnout is a state of emotional, mental, and often physical exhaustion brought on by prolonged or repeated stress. Though it is most often caused by problems at work, it can also appear in other areas of life, such as parenting, caretaking, or romantic relationships." The Mayo Clinic explains it this way:

> Job burnout is a type of stress linked to work. It includes being worn out physically or emotionally. Job burnout may also involve feeling useless, powerless, and empty. Burnout isn't a medical diagnosis. Some experts think that other conditions, such as depression, are behind burnout. Burnout can raise the risk of depression. But depression and burnout are different, and they need different treatments. Certain personality traits may affect the risk of burnout. Other factors, such as past work experiences, also can affect burnout risk. That helps explain why if two people are dealing with the same issues, one might have job burnout while the other does not.

Stress and burnout manifest in different ways. According to the American Psychological Association (APA), stress is "The physiological or psychological response to internal or external stressors. Stress involves changes affecting nearly every body system, influencing how people feel and behave. For example, it may manifest in palpitations, sweating, dry mouth, shortness of breath, fidgeting, accelerated speech, augmentation of negative emotions (if already experienced), and longer duration of stress fatigue. The general adaptation syndrome manifests severe stress. By causing these mind-body changes, stress contributes directly to psychological and physiological disorders and diseases and affects mental and physical health, reducing the quality of life."[xxvi]

Stress has its advantages and disadvantages. According to *Psychology Today*:

> …the psychological perception of pressure and the body's response to it involves multiple systems, from metabolism to muscles to memory. It can be necessary for survival but also harmful. Many people today feel they perpetually struggle with stress and anxiety. Society's obsession with productivity, the steady stream of digital information we consume, increasingly sedentary lifestyles, and feelings of overwhelm may contribute to the stress that so many are feeling. Short bursts of stress aren't inherently harmful, although it can take time for the body to calm down. Yet prolonged or repeated arousal of the stress response can have harmful physical and psychological consequences. Those repercussions include ailments from

heart disease and diabetes to anxiety and depression. Stress can lead to changes in many different parts of the body. Stress can lead to a faster heartbeat, muscle tension, and gastrointestinal issues. It can lead to heavier and faster breathing, which can strain the lungs and blunt the immune system's ability to respond to threats. Ongoing stress assaults the immune system, making us more vulnerable to disease. Although stress hormones prepare the body for emergencies, they depress the immune system by decreasing inflammation and white blood cell production. Stress may, therefore, contribute to illnesses such as heart disease, cancer, and others. Stress hormones, such as cortisol, are naturally produced daily so that people can take on the challenges ahead. But marinating in high levels of stress hormones over time can prompt the brain to function differently, leading to memory impairment, cognitive problems, anxiety, or depression.[xxx]

According to the World Health Organization, these are some signs of stress:

Stress makes it hard for us to relax and can come with a range of emotions, including anxiety and irritability. When stressed, we may find it difficult to concentrate. We may experience headaches, other body pains, an upset stomach, or trouble sleeping. We may have lost our appetite or eaten more than usual. Chronic stress can worsen pre-existing health problems and may increase our use of alcohol, tobacco, and other substances.[xxxi]

While the preceding focuses on the effects of stress, the American Psychological Association—style guide (APA) defines burnout, on the other hand, as physical, emotional, or mental exhaustion accompanied by decreased motivation, lowered performance, and negative attitudes toward oneself and others. It results from high performance until stress and tension, especially from extreme and prolonged physical or mental exertion or an overburdening workload, take their toll. The word was first used in this sense in 1975 by U.S. psychologist Herbert J. Freudenberger (1926–1999) in referring to workers in clinics with heavy caseloads.

Burnout is most often observed in professionals who work in service-oriented vocations (e.g., social workers, teachers, correctional officers) and experience chronic high levels of stress. It can be particularly acute in therapists or counselors doing trauma work, who feel overwhelmed by the cumulative secondary trauma of witnessing the effects. Burnout is also experienced by athletes when continually exposed to stress associated with performance without commensurate rewards or rest.[xxxii]

The National Institute of Health shares the list of possible signs of burnout below. All definitions of burnout given so far share the idea that the symptoms are thought to be caused by work-related or other kinds of stress. One example of a source of stress outside of work is caring for a family member. Three main areas of symptoms are considered signs of burnout:

- **Exhaustion:** People affected feel drained and emotionally exhausted, unable to cope, tired and down, and lacking energy. Physical symptoms include pain and gastrointestinal (stomach or bowel) problems.

- **Alienation from (work-related) activities:** People who have burnout find their jobs increasingly stressful and frustrating. They may start being cynical about their working conditions and their colleagues. At the same time, they may increasingly distance themselves emotionally and start feeling numb about their work.

- **Reduced performance:** Burnout mainly affects everyday tasks at work, home, or when caring for family members. People with burnout are very negative about their tasks, find it hard to concentrate, are listless, and lack creativity.

As an individual who has experienced burnout and is still recovering from it, I can recognize the patterns of burnout in high-achieving immigrant women. I come across these women frequently and have discovered that they all have one thing in common: juggling multiple projects, whether it be work, extracurricular activities, or social events. They are highly committed to their family of origin and nuclear family and are often seen as alpha females or matriarchs of the family. These women struggle with balancing self-care, setting boundaries, and determining how much they can handle. I can relate to this struggle because I am one of these women. I have witnessed burnout up close and find that high-achieving immigrant women, in particular, struggle severely with it. One reason for this is that mental health discussions are often taboo in many collectivist cultures and immigrant settings. Seeking mental health support is viewed as a sign of being 'crazy,' and admitting that you need help can be accompanied by feelings of shame and guilt. This is often due to the belief that your parents carried so much and did so much with less, so you should be able to handle everything independently.

There is also the dynamic of the struggle that comes with balancing cultural expectations of family and community back home, as well as becoming a hybrid of the previous birth country and the now adopted country.

The struggle is real.

You are choosing and negotiating what parts of the previous culture fall away or remain within you and what parts of the new culture you will adopt and become part of your identity—the isolation from and clinging to the validation of people of the birth country. Negotiating which part of a new cultural identity and people will influence who you become. Letting go of certain relationships from previous cultures that no longer serve you or where you have come to realize do not support who you truly are at the core and wish to become. This can be a painful experience. You have a long history with some of these relationships. Still, recognizing that to integrate balance in your current state of affairs, you must evaluate which relationships are healthy and unhealthy. This may mean letting go of dear aunty, uncle, cousin, neighbor, or others who seem to keep you tethered to the old behaviors and patterns that you are so desperate to free yourself from to become who you need to become to survive in this new culture/world/society. Here is something to ponder: would you rather be at war within and at peace with the world or at war with the world and at peace within?

The regular daily stresses of life heightened by an intense job, cultural expectations, and responsibilities all contribute to burnout—the constant striving. You cannot rest or release the mental load of responsibility/burden of the former culture and life. These old relationships will remind you, shame you, or use guilt to get you to play the old roles where they are comfortable with you and may benefit from you continuing. You cannot do this alone. It would be best if you had a support, accountability group - people who understand the struggles you are experiencing and can allow you to be your authentic self even in overwhelming emotions. People with cultural competence. Therapists with cultural competence. Coaches with cultural competence. I have encountered many so-called coaches on the general market who lack cultural understanding of their clients. They may have clinical training (therapists and counselors/social workers) and social awareness of possible issues, but cultural understanding and experience are often missing. Many are mentors or consultants but not coaches. Now more than ever, we need coaching, therapists, and medical providers with intercultural competence to deliver targeted care to diverse clients.

How Burnout Affects Women

Becoming a human-doing is quite beneficial for a capitalistic society/economy, but does it serve you? I know this may seem to come from a place of privilege, but honestly, ask yourself this question. I get that many immigrants do not have the luxury to ponder such questions as they have mouths to feed at home and back home. The hustle is real. I get that you are so energized to finally be in the land that flows with milk and honey and roads paved with gold, and you only want to apply your energies, skills, and ingenuity to get a piece of the proverbial pie. After all, everyone at home and back home depends on you. The pressure to succeed and avoid mistakes is immense. One that no one who has not walked the immigrant journey will be able to understand and relate to. Do you have to sacrifice yourself to pursue success, or is there a wiser path to find alignment and joy with your career path that would keep you healthy and likely "make room" for your inevitable success, i.e., working in passion? Do you have to be an engineer, lawyer, or doctor? Will you end up miserable after investing many years into studying for a career that possibly destroys your health, relationships, and well-being? A word of caution to all workaholics from another world: you do not have to let go of the being from the collectivistic culture to become a human-doing. The sweet spot is in an integrated balance of the collectivist and the individualistic (obsessive productivity-driven) cultures. It is possible to create balance in chasing the American Dream. You do not have to destroy yourself in the process. If you struggle to find balance, set boundaries, or recognize the choices and possibilities for a more integrated life, connect with our team to schedule a coaching session. You will be happy you did.

CHAPTER 8

There is No Place Like Home;
There's No Place Like Home.
—Dorothy, Wizard of Oz

I Have Become a Foreigner in the Land of my Birth

Have your attempts to escape ceased? I am still searching. I have made great strides in surrendering to the possibility that the U.S. may become my home for now. For the longest time, I envisioned marrying and raising children in Jamaica. That was the mental frame and experience I had to draw on. My previous teachers poured their hearts, love, and passion for learning into us. I am forever grateful to them. It is sad to hear stories of immigrant children or children of immigrants who are not receiving a similar experience in the educational system here in this country, where teachers expect too little of their students. Teachers take teaching jobs because it is a means to an end to pay off university debt or something else. Parts of me still long for the life I had back on the island. I have memories of a happy childhood, my mind being stretched by educators, and a sense of belonging I have never found since leaving. Losing one's cultural self and sense of belonging can be painful and disorienting. I am still making sense of it.

I have realized that things have changed on the island since I was a young version of myself. Albeit that, I may be holding onto a fantasized version of the island that no longer exists. The economy, politics, education, nutritional diet, media exposure, social scenes, and so much have changed over the last two decades. I remember when the Jamaican dollar was JMD\$7 to USD\$1, and today, it ebbs around JMD\$ 140-150 to USD\$1. I remember the older folks being die-hard supporters of a particular party and the younger generation (me included) dreaming of younger blood entering the political space. I was elated when Andrew Holness won his first election. Friends tell me that students have changed and are highly influenced by social media and consume much of the U.S. media production via cable TV and other platforms. The culture has changed. Eating at fast food places is now cool, which was frowned upon during my younger days. To my surprise, during a recent visit, Jamaica now has Dunkin Donuts, Popeyes, and other fast food chains that were never on the island. I observed lines wrapped around the building, pulling up to a drive-thru. Can anyone foresee this impact on the island's overall nutrition and traditional healthy diet? I see young people donning how cool it is and being proud to eat at Kentucky Fried Chicken (KFC) and these other fast food spots.

The island I experienced during my formative years is a different place. There may be pockets of people still holding to the traditional Jamaican diet, educational prowess, and social goings and comings. Still, the next generation of Jamaicans is being influenced by the outside at a level never before seen during our time. Many have noted, and I observed, that the resort industry has opted to cater heavily toward the American palette. I do not know about you, but when I travel, I expect to experience the local culture, including the local cuisine, not poor food options from the place where I just left. Some tourists complained about few American food options, so the resorts pivoted. At the hotel's buffet, I noticed a corner dedicated to local Jamaican cuisine, and the rest of the dining room was filled with American options like bagels, donuts, and bread. It seems that complaints prompted the resorts to switch back to offering mostly local Jamaican cuisine, though I have not verified it. Safety and security appear to have been a central issue. As trafficking in persons has become a global phenomenon, Jamaica has not escaped being impacted. I heard of a young lady being picked up by a taxi driver, and she was present while the driver discussed and negotiated the price at which she would be sold to another.

The stories are unending and worrisome. One has to consider the realities of now being in the group known as 'returning residents.' Many people are returning to the island, including people native to other places. Real estate has been booming in Jamaica more recently than ever before. The Ambassador reports that the Jamaica "brand" is ranked in the top ten worldwide, so the tourism industry is doing its job. It is, however, essential to consider what the dynamic of a returning resident could potentially be. How will your previous friends, neighbors, and others view you? How safe will you be? Would you need to change your social circle? Who will now become your inner circle in the place you were born and once lived? These ponderings flow through me periodically as I try to make sense of my roots and where will be my next 'home.' So, is Jamaica still home? I still have fond memories of growing up on our family properties (both sides), which are still there and thriving. What will happen to these lands and family plots? What will become of the family properties now that grandmas and grandpas have transitioned to the realm of the ancestors? Who will care for the property, pay taxes, and many other questions? This is to be uncovered. One thing, though, I have surrendered to decoding the U.S. and possibly calling this home, at least for the next decade. Nevertheless, I dream of a beachfront home with white sand beach, flavorful foods, fresh produce, plants, daily sunlight, and that cool breeze relaxing my vibration. I am still seeking that elusive place where all my attempts to escape come to an end.

I have become a foreigner in the place I once called home. Have you ever had this realization? This has hit me harder in 2023 than in previous encounters with the island. I went back for mango season over the Summer of 2023 as I had longed for this experience my entire time here in the U.S. Would you believe that a memory from childhood stayed with me this long? As I entered the mango walk and reached out to pick a mango, the immediate smell of the stem leaving the tree transported me back to my younger days. I exclaimed, "This is where this memory took place. I could not remember, but the smell brought it all back." As I inhaled mango after mango, my senses came alive. The hairs on my skin rose, and a sense of fulfillment and joy washed over me. I found it. I validated the joyful memory of eating mangos again. A sense of peace came over me as I walked from tree to tree, handpicking mangos and sharing the experience with our daughter. There were green mangos, red and yellow mangos. Excitement overwhelmed me as I took in the scenery and looked around at the homes nestled in nooks and crannies of the surrounding mountain peaks draped in the foggy, fresh morning air.

After living in bustling cities and experiencing so many anxieties from whistling fire trucks, police cars, trains, and more, I have come to long for and better appreciate the peace I felt in those wrapping hills. I daydreamed of what it would be like to wake up to this tranquility every morning, the sounds of roosters, goats, birds, cows, and donkeys announcing the arrival of a new day. As we drove back to Mom's family property, I thought of the fact that she was no longer physically present so that I could share that experience with her. She lay resting next to her parents and sister. I felt gratitude, and a sense of perspective rested over me. I was glad that we took Mom home during the height of the COVID-19 shutdown when the Jamaican government restricted funerals to 20 people. We were not allowed to attend the church funeral but settled on a tent outside the family home, a screen showing memories and surrounded by the embrace of those few who risked leaving their home during a pandemic. Mom was home. How could I bury her in a foreign land? I felt peace knowing I had done the last right thing to honor her. Despite the bickering and unhelpful talk, I stood firm. Mom was finally home where her memories and roots ran deep, in the cool air nestled under a June Plum tree, several breadfruit trees, mango trees, and more, enveloping her with an everlasting shade. Mom was finally home.

Re-Entry Shock/Reverse Culture Shock/Psychological Disorientation Brought on by Foreign Experiences

Re-entry shock, also known as reverse culture shock, occurs when immigrants return to their home country after an extended period abroad. This phenomenon can be surprisingly challenging as individuals struggle to readjust to a once-familiar environment. The shock arises from changes in the home country, shifts in personal identity, and altered perspectives developed during the time abroad. Common symptoms include feelings of alienation, frustration, and confusion as the returnees navigate different cultural norms and expectations. The dissonance between memories and current realities can lead to a sense of disorientation and emotional discomfort, making re-entry a complex and sometimes difficult transition.

Cultural Homelessness/Third-Culture Experience

How did I become a foreigner in the land of my birth? I go to the store and the market, and people tell me: "don't say anything; I will negotiate." I tried to speak patios, but my accent has changed due to learning Spanish and French, living in Mexico City for two years, and picking up the Spanish accent. It has changed due to living in the U.S. and adopting the way I speak to sound more American so people could understand me better and stop asking me to repeat myself. I had left what I knew to go to a new land where I had to assimilate to thrive. That choice led to the distance created between the people and places that once oozed from my pores.

After my birthday summer trip, I listened to a podcast hosted by a local Jamaican and found myself reveling in her accent and saddened by the fact that I no longer sounded that way. I cried. That feeling sat over me for days and weeks and still surfaces. This is who I am. This is where I was born. I still eat Jamaican food, and after trying foods from most countries worldwide, I still come home to the Jamaican taste every day. There is nothing like it to me. I often get disappointed when I go to restaurants, so I try to cook as often as possible at home. Finding healthy food in the U.S. has been quite challenging for me. It is unsafe to eat just anything or stop at any fast food joint. Every time I do, I end up paying the price. I have learned my lesson, and now I abstain from unhealthy eating to maintain my gut health, maintain a healthy weight, and rest well at night.

Once back in the U.S., I was never accepted as an American. Black Americans do not accept me because I somehow do not fit in. White American neither because I do not have the phenotype. Jamaicans who are 'fresh off the boat' because, well, I have changed and appear too American for them. Where do I belong? My search for belonging as an immigrant continues after two decades. Not being accepted by any one group can be painful. Too proper and not Black enough for some. Too melanated for some, hair not straight enough for others, accent too thick for some. I am now a hybrid of the Jamaican culture and the American culture. I found that these 'hybrids' are my people: those who have walked this road, have adopted new cultural norms, adapted to different environments, and lived in other places are Third-Culture People and cultural bridge people. These are the people with whom I fit. Now I am searching for them. I feel most at home and have a sense of belonging among them. My search for a home continues. The phenomenon where immigrants feel they do not fit into either their new adopted country or their birth country is known as "cultural homelessness" or "third-culture experience." This experience can lead to a profound sense of dislocation and identity confusion.

The Transformative Journey of Immigrants: Navigating Identity and Heritage

The immigration experience is one of profound change, encompassing psychological, social, economic, and cultural dimensions. Let us explore the multifaceted transformations immigrants undergo after moving abroad, focusing on their adaptation processes, the impact on their identity, and the balance between retaining their roots and integrating into a new society.

Acculturation and Adaptation

Acculturation, the process of adopting the cultural norms and values of the host country, is a central aspect of the immigrant experience. Psychologist John Berry's acculturation model provides a useful framework for understanding this process. Berry identifies four primary acculturation strategies:

1. Assimilation: Immigrants abandon their original culture and fully embrace the host culture. This strategy often involves adopting new social norms, learning the host country's language, and modifying daily practices to align with those of the new society.

2. Integration: Immigrants maintain aspects of their original culture while also adopting parts of the host culture. This bicultural approach can lead to a more enriched identity and a smoother adaptation process.

3. Separation: Immigrants retain their original culture and reject the host culture. This strategy can result in strong cultural preservation but may also lead to social isolation.

4. Marginalization: Immigrants neither maintain their original culture nor adopt the host culture. This strategy is often associated with feelings of alienation and can lead to negative psychological outcomes.

Psychological Impact

The psychological effects of acculturation are significant. Immigrants often face challenges related to identity and self-esteem as they navigate their new environment.

- Identity and Self-Esteem: Assimilation can sometimes lead to a loss of identity and lower self-esteem, as immigrants may feel disconnected from their heritage and the new culture. Conversely, integration can foster a strong bicultural identity and higher self-esteem, providing a sense of belonging in both worlds.

- Stress and Mental Health: Acculturative stress is a common experience for immigrants, manifesting as anxiety, depression, and other mental health issues. Effective support systems and coping mechanisms are essential for mitigating these effects and promoting psychological well-being.

Social Dynamics

Social interactions and networks play a crucial role in the adaptation process of immigrants.

- Social Networks: Initially, immigrants often rely on co-ethnic networks for support. Over time, many form new social ties with members of the host society. The extent and nature of these networks significantly impact their adaptation and overall experience.

- Discrimination and Prejudice: Experiences of discrimination can hinder the acculturation process and negatively affect psychological well-being. Positive social interactions and inclusive environments in the host society are critical for facilitating smoother adaptation and fostering a sense of belonging.

Cultural Retention vs. Cultural Loss

Balancing cultural retention and adapting to the host culture is a complex and personal process for immigrants.

- **Cultural Practices:** Immigrants may retain cultural practices such as cuisine, festivals, and religious observances. However, the pressure to conform to the host culture can sometimes lead to the erosion of these practices.

- **Language:** Retaining the native language is a key aspect of cultural preservation. Immigrants often face the challenge of maintaining their heritage language while learning a new language. Second-generation immigrants are particularly at risk of losing their native language, highlighting the importance of language retention efforts.

Economic and Educational Outcomes

Successful economic and educational integration is vital for the long-term well-being of immigrants.

- **Economic Integration:** Navigating the host country's labor market often requires retraining, credential recognition, and adapting to workplace cultures. Successful economic integration is associated with better overall adaptation and quality of life.

- **Educational Attainment:** The educational outcomes of immigrant children can be influenced by the level of cultural and social integration. Bicultural competence often correlates with better educational outcomes, highlighting the importance of supportive educational environments.

Long-Term Changes

Over generations, the immigrant experience evolves, with significant inter-generational changes in cultural identity and integration.

- **Intergenerational Changes:** Over time, there is typically a shift towards greater integration or assimilation. Second-generation immigrants often experience a dual identity, balancing both their heritage and host cultures. This dynamic can enrich their cultural experience but also present unique challenges.

- **Cultural Hybridity:** Immigrants and their descendants may develop a hybrid culture, blending elements of both their heritage and the host cultures. This cultural hybridity reflects the evolving nature of immigrant identities and their ongoing adaptation process.

Resilience and Coping Mechanisms

Immigrants often display remarkable resilience and adaptability as they navigate the challenges of living in a new country:

- **Adaptability:** Immigrants develop various strategies to cope with the complexities of their new environment. This adaptability is crucial for overcoming challenges and achieving successful integration.
- **Support Systems:** The presence of supportive community networks, both from their own ethnic group and the broader society, is vital for successful adaptation. These networks provide essential resources, emotional support, and a sense of belonging.

The transformative journey of immigrants involves navigating a complex interplay of retaining their heritage and adapting to a new culture. This process is highly individual, influenced by personal resilience, social support, and the socio-political context of the host country. Research highlights the importance of supportive policies and inclusive practices in facilitating positive outcomes for immigrants. By understanding these dynamics, each country can better appreciate the rich and diverse contributions that immigrants bring to their new societies and the ongoing evolution of their identities.

Not all that Glitters is Gold

Is it ever the right thing to put collective needs over the personal?

Are you so focused on the needs of people back home that you neglect the people around you who are supporting you?

You will have nothing left in your tank or resources to give back to these people. I have been exploring this idea for some time. To find the right balance, one has to come home to oneself to integrate the right balance.

Have you ever noticed that you are missing what is happening in the present but that your day has much to do with mental narratives (i.e., thoughts about things)? Either remembering the past or daydreaming about the future but never the present. Something happens, and immediately, you start interpreting what just happened and wonder why he/she/they did that. What caused that? Who did that? What were they thinking? There are so many thoughts surrounding everything you notice. Your day goes from one thought to the next. Have you ever wondered, "What did I miss today because I was so preoccupied with thoughts of yesterday, the next meeting, or what needs to be done at home or tomorrow for a child's rehearsal? Often, we are plagued with worry, fear, memories of yesterday, and anticipation of the future. Our perception of life is what we are experiencing rather than the realities taking place. Do you ever slow down to just BE here now? This occurred to me recently, and I have tried to practice being here now as I was missing out on what was happening in my life, such as:

- Life is beautiful and peaceful.
- Life is filled with joy and goodness.
- If I slowed down to smell the roses, I could notice the joy within me in the simple things.
- I did not need to chase another accomplishment to fill me as that would only provide momentary fulfillment.
- The joys and goodness I sought were already within me. I did not need to achieve anything to finally see them.
- Joy is not a pursuit, for all I needed and sought could be found in stillness, the thing this culture seems to be afraid of and is running from.

I decided after Mom passed on January 1, 2021, that I would return to the essence of my being because the chasing had not brought me fulfillment. I had spent two decades studying and achieving, stacking up accolades, awards, and travel miles, but missing time with the woman who brought me into this realm. As the reality that she was no longer present to talk with hit me, all of the aforementioned feelings came rushing in. What was all the achieving for if it took me away from the people I cared about the most and wanted to make proud and support? I had lost myself in the doing. I had lost sight of the essential, the significance, the meaning of my life here in the U.S.

I had become a human-doing.

I sometimes find it hard to slow down and be with the people around me. I was physically present, but my mind was elsewhere or running from dysfunctional behaviors I observed in others. All along, the peace, the joy, the acceptance, and the resolve I pursued were already within me. I had thought it was in going to church to listen to a pastor preach about how good God is to us and how to appease this God to protect and provide. All external to me. One day, I realized that I had arrived here from the creator, and the creator had never left me. In my deepest essence, nothing in this world could touch me. As the Bible says, "Neither life nor death nor anything can separate us from the love of God." The creator has guided, protected, led, and directed me from then until now.

Where did we all get taught that we are sinful and bad to the core? You are not a beast, a monster, or a devil. You are not rotten at the core. From whence did this idea start? That sinful nature that everyone seems to be so afraid of looking straight in the eye. We all arrived here as innocent babies. We picked up any thinking or mind activity currently flowing through us here. Sounds like this is nurture, not nature, to me.

Looking Within

Why are many so scared to slow down and look within? We will use any number of activities, behaviors, and soothers to sedate us and avoid not looking at ourselves as we are. You come from pure innocence and pure goodness, and that is who you are in your essence. The thoughts or mental conditioning that flow through you are not you but simply instructions from the mind to protect you or teach you how to survive here. Tap into your superpower, your connection to the divine, and stop allowing people to talk you out of your power. The goodness of God has always been within you and me. We were, at birth, conditioned to think in a certain way and give up the power that was always inside. Peace, joy, and fulfillment are not without; it is within. I was tired of external conditioning and finally recognized that peace, joy, belonging, and more were always there, but the noisy, conditioned mind blocked that from coming forth. All the noisy conditioning is what blocked the spirit of the divine creator from manifesting the will and purpose of my life here. Once I realized that I was getting in my own way, I surrendered. This is how I came home to myself and determined to allow the power of God to flow through uninterrupted and untethered to the mental conditionings of the human world.

We take our consciousness wherever we go. Wherever we are, our mind and consciousness are. Those are the things that we dwell on or think about. I clearly remember having strong desires to go back home. Then, one day, I realized I was trying to run from the harsh environment of the United States. This can be a cruel place for a person of African descent. In addition, as I saw the realities of the collective psyche, mindset, and realities playing out on social media, news, and other platforms, I did not want to be a part of it. There is a certain madness about what we see reported or shared. I prefer to be in a collective where people are more connected to their being's essence and not human doings. From person to person, it appeared that people would sacrifice each other to achieve any goal. The WIIFM mentality was deeply entrenched in the culture and unattractive. I wanted to run to another land. I wanted to run away. I did not want to raise our daughter here. Her autopilot mind is being set in the first few years. I was concerned about the conditioning that would become a part of her subconscious mind just by being in and around certain behaviors or environments.

Then, one day, I realized I could not run from myself.

We take our consciousness wherever we go. Those are the things that we dwell on or think about. The reality of what I was observing was often true, but my perception of that reality also made it appear worse. I would travel to different environments and notice undesirable things as well. Where will I ever go and not see undesirable behaviors or environments on this planet?   I cannot continue to run from myself even though it appears that the ugly side of humanity is everywhere. That was not actual reality. Beautiful human beings were behaving in conscious ways around me. Energy flows where attention goes. If I continued to ponder and think about the undesirable things, I would continue to see more of them. I was like a magnet for the things I did not want because they flowed across my thinking and frequently bothered me.

What if I could dwell on the things I desire more?

What if I could become more aware of the thoughts flowing unconsciously through me, erase those as much as possible, clear the cache, and meditate on the happy thoughts, the joyful thoughts, and the beauty I would see around me? The same should be true. I could attract more of this goodness to my every reality. No matter what country, city, town, or planet I am physically on. The world happens within us. Not without us. This revolutionized the way I saw things. I do have some control of the world I created from my mind station. Finally, I realized that I had a superpower. I was not this helpless being here to take what life handed me. Yes, there are things out of our control, but through meditation and intentionally observing my thoughts, activities, and patterns, I could change the way I experience the world. No one else can do this for me but me.

Stop giving up your power.

Come Home to Yourself and Realize the Power you have Within

What does it mean to come home to oneself? Let us review:

The atmosphere, things, and people around us change when we change. Have you ever noticed that you can hunger for someone's attention, validation from someone you admire or love, or some unnamed thing or experience? That is our soul and heart trying to get our attention.

The answers to all we need are within us. Not without us.

I have played with this realization for some time. Peace automatically follows whenever I settle down, care for myself, and fill up my cup with whatever my soul craves. I go within and see what life is mirroring to me and watch as all my need for external validation subsides. The moment you are full and realize you are wholly enough, in and through and all around, the thing you were aching for, yearning for, hungering for, and longing for shows up.

Isn't life funny? I am not quite sure what exactly it is. Still, I have come across many folks talking about the law of attraction, and my only explanation is that once you recognize that nothing out there can fill you, you are enough because you are enough in your deeper self. Not in your physical form but in your soul. That you are lacking nothing. Then those things suddenly attract you and somehow find their way to you. When we change, the things and people around us change. I have tried for so long to help people change, nudge people to change, to improve, and to want more. It has been an utter waste of my energy and frustrated me to the nth degree. No one will change until they are ready to change. Focus your energy on changing, improving, and refining who you are. Those who want to change, when and if they are ready, will ask how you did it or learn by just watching, seeing how you changed, or reading about it, BUT only if and when they are ready. The same divine wisdom and intelligence guide everyone. Why should you use your limited energy trying to convince someone to change? Learn from me and save yourself the headache.

Coming home to yourself means letting go of the collectivist cultural pressure to get people to improve, change, and want more for themselves. That is the "maximizer" in me (from the Clifton Strengths Finder). Clifton Strengths, formerly known as StrengthsFinder, is a personal development and performance-enhancement tool developed by Gallup. The tool is designed to help individuals identify their unique strengths and leverage them for personal and professional growth. Here are some key points about Clifton Strengths. Created by Dr. Donald O. Clifton, a psychologist and researcher, Clifton Strengths is based on the idea that focusing on strengths rather than weaknesses leads to higher performance and greater personal fulfillment. Dr. Clifton is often referred to as the father of strengths-based psychology. The Clifton Strengths assessment is an online tool that measures an individual's natural patterns of thinking, feeling, and behaving. It consists of a series of questions that help identify a person's top strengths out of a possible 34 themes. The 34 themes, also known as talent themes or strengths, are categorized into four domains:

- **Executing:** Themes that help make things happen.
- **Influencing:** Themes that help take charge, speak up, and ensure others are heard.

- **Relationship Building:** Themes that help build strong relationships and hold a team together.
- **Strategic Thinking:** Themes that help analyze and understand complex situations and concepts.

After completing the assessment (https://www.gallup.com/cliftonstrengths/en/home.aspx), individuals receive a detailed report highlighting their top five strengths (with the option to unlock all 34). According to Clifton, he report includes insights into how these strengths manifest in their lives and practical advice on applying them effectively. Clifton Strengths is widely used in various settings, including:

- **Personal Development:** Helping individuals understand and maximize their potential.
- **Professional Development:** Enhancing performance and satisfaction at work.
- **Team Building:** Improving team dynamics and collaboration by recognizing and leveraging the diverse strengths of team members.
- **Leadership Development:** Helping leaders understand their strengths and how to lead more effectively.

The philosophy behind Clifton Strengths is that individuals gain more by building on their strengths rather than trying to fix their weaknesses. This approach encourages people to focus on what they naturally do well and develop those areas further. Overall, Clifton Strengths provides a positive and empowering framework for personal and professional growth, emphasizing the development of inherent talents into strengths. This assessment has helped me better understand how I show up in the world, interact with others and to zoom in and maximize the strengths area inherent to me and my life experience versus spending diminishing returns on working on weaknesses which can zap motivation and drive. That is using carrots rather than sticks, starting from a place of power rather than lack. According to Clifton Strengths, People with the Maximizer strength focus on transforming something strong into something superb. They seek to maximize their talents and the talents of others, striving for excellence and continuously improving.

Here are the key characteristics and behaviors associated with the Maximizer strength: The Maximizer strength is one of the 34 talent themes identified by the Clifton Strengths assessment. People with the Maximizer strength focus on transforming something strong into something superb. They seek to maximize their talents and the talents of others, striving for excellence and continuously improving.

Here are the key characteristics and behaviors associated with the Maximizer strength: Focus on Strengths: Maximizers concentrate on their strengths and the strengths of others. They are keenly aware of their own talents and are drawn to tasks and roles where they can utilize these strengths to achieve outstanding results.

Quality Orientation: People with the Maximizer theme strongly desire excellence. They are unsatisfied with good or average performance; they aim for the best possible outcomes.

Efficiency: Maximizers are efficient in their approach. They understand that focusing on strengths is a more effective use of time and resources than trying to improve weaknesses.

Inspiring Others: Maximizers often inspire and motivate others to develop and use their strengths. They can identify others' strengths and help them see how these strengths can be further developed and applied.

Preference for Excellence: Maximizers are attracted to excellence and tend to surround themselves with people, products, and experiences they consider the best. They prefer high quality over high quantity.

Continuous Improvement: They always look for ways to improve good things. This drive for continuous improvement can lead to innovations and advancements in their personal and professional lives.

Strengths-Based Development: Maximizers are advocates of strengths-based development, believing that honing and leveraging one's strengths leads to greater success and satisfaction. In practical terms, someone with the Maximizer strength might excel in roles where they can mentor or coach others, lead projects to higher standards, or continuously improve processes and outcomes. They thrive in environments that value and reward high performance and quality.

Being Right vs Being Joyful

"If you think something is good or bad, either way, you are right." The Bible says, "For as he thinketh in his heart, so is he." (Proverbs 23:7 KJV). Do you care about being right or being at peace? It's one of the great mysteries of life. This is what it feels like to come home to yourself. To recognize that nothing out there, from anyone, from any place, nothing anyone says, does, does not do, or does not say takes anything from you.

You are divine. You are enough. You are full. You are lacking nothing.

If you are agnostic, this book is not for you. This is for those who can sense or believe in a greater intelligence, something greater than themselves. You came from the creator, from the source, lacking nothing. The mental conditioning of our environments, such as capitalism and consumerism, teaches us that we are lacking something and need someone or something else to complete us or make us feel whole. Coming home to yourself means finally maturing and taking full responsibility for your life, actions, and decisions. Coming home to yourself stops the blame game for past harm, trauma, or anything you feel you were deprived of and fully embrace all of life today. You do have the power to make decisions over what happens to you now, in the present, about what does not serve you. It can feel like we are doomed to continue living in the memory of pain, trauma, regret, and whatever is holding us back, but it is possible to clear the cache. Take your power back today. You are not helpless. Come home to yourself.

Coming Home to Yourself Means that You Mature into Who You Were Meant to Be

Coming home to yourself means you take full responsibility for your actions or inactions. You release your parents for their actions or inactions and forgive your family of origin, extended family, or anyone else. You set boundaries on people's demands on your time, resources or the sovereignty of who you are. You start saying no to making space for yourself so that you can heal. You say no so that you can make space to quiet yourself, to go within to become aware of the creator's purpose/will for you being here.

This culture in the United States is one of constant doing. We must be careful not to lose our sense of being in this constant on-the-go culture. It is in quietness that we find direction. It is in slowing down that we recognize that the answer was always there within us all along. If we stop and observe, the times when we seek external validation or confirmation are the times when we are least home with ourselves.

We can learn and be inspired by each other's journeys, but we are each powerfully equipped to solve, heal ourselves (if we listen to our guidance system), and find peace and joy within. It is amazing that despite the wealth in this country, people are likely more unhappy than in countries that appear to have less. How could this be? Are people happier in collectivist cultures than in individualistic cultures? The relationship between cultural orientation (collectivist vs. individualistic) and happiness is complex and influenced by multiple factors. Research in this area provides insights into how cultural values and social structures impact overall well-being and happiness.

Collectivist Cultures

1. **Social Support and Community:** People in collectivist cultures often experience strong social support from family and community. This support can lead to higher levels of well-being and happiness due to the sense of belonging and security it provides.

2. **Interdependence and Cooperation:** Emphasizing interdependence and cooperation can foster a sense of harmony and reduce conflict, contributing positively to overall happiness.

3. **Life Satisfaction:** In collectivist societies, life satisfaction is often derived from fulfilling social roles and responsibilities, maintaining family harmony, and contributing to the community.

Individualistic Cultures

1. **Autonomy and Freedom:** Individualistic cultures emphasize personal autonomy, freedom of choice, and self-expression, which can lead to higher levels of personal satisfaction and happiness for many individuals.

2. **Achievement and Personal Goals:** Happiness in individualistic cultures is often linked to personal achievements, success, and the fulfillment of individual goals and desires.

3. **Diverse Social Networks:** While social support may be less intense than in collectivist cultures, individuals in individualistic societies often have diverse social networks that can provide emotional and practical support.

Comparative Studies and Findings

- **Subjective Well-Being:** Studies have shown mixed results regarding subjective well-being (SWB) in collectivist and individualistic cultures. Some research indicates that people in individualistic cultures report higher levels of SWB due to the emphasis on personal achievement and freedom. However, other studies suggest that collectivist cultures report higher life satisfaction due to strong social support networks.

- **Cultural Adaptation:** People's happiness may also depend on how well they adapt to the dominant cultural norms. Individuals who align with their society's cultural values tend to report higher levels of happiness.

- **Economic Factors:** Economic stability and prosperity play a significant role in determining happiness. Wealthier individualistic societies might report higher levels of happiness due to better access to resources and opportunities.

- **Value of Relationships:** In collectivist cultures, the quality and depth of relationships often take precedence over individual achievements, which can lead to a different, equally valid form of happiness compared to individualistic cultures.

There is no definitive answer as to whether people are happier in collectivist or individualistic cultures because happiness is multifaceted and influenced by numerous factors, including cultural values, economic conditions, social support, and individual personality traits. Both cultural orientations offer unique pathways to happiness, and the effectiveness of these pathways can vary based on individual preferences and societal context.

We often hear stories from highly successful people that, despite having the proverbial everything, they are not happy due to acquiring things or more wealth. Yet, we can observe people from countries who, by the standards of the United States, have less but are more peaceful, joyful, and connected to their inner essence. Is it possible to find that balance as an immigrant-American? We arrived from the collectivist to the individualistic and have experienced both. I believe this is part of our superpower: we know both worlds intricately. We can balance the desire for self-gratification against the desire to be altruistic and have community impact. Perhaps an ideal for someone born in a collectivist culture could be a hybrid of space for individual aspiration coupled with some level of cooperation, social support, and healthy community interaction.

Coming home to ourselves means we allow space for and welcome our healthy selves

Our responses and reactions often stem solely from our perceptions of what is happening around us. Have you ever stopped, gone within, and observed whether you were responding to reality or perception (thoughts about things)?

Coming home to ourselves means that we slow down and go within, face the good, bad, and ugly, and offer grace and love to ourselves. In finding our own healing, we are likely to then offer that same grace and love to another. It is likely impossible to offer grace, peace, and love to one another while there is a war going on inside. This is true self-acceptance when we can come home and accept everything about ourselves. It all starts within and through us. The more we heal, the more healing flows from us to others. World peace begins with us. World peace happens inside each of us before it is extended outside us to our families, friends, and wider community and world.

Coming home to yourself means seeing the acres of diamonds around you and overcoming a scarcity mindset.

Coming home means going from surviving to thriving. This means allowing yourself to drop, release, and let go of the habits, behaviors, and roles that no longer serve you. You begin to allow yourself to work smarter, not harder.

Coming home to yourself means letting go of your way (automatic thoughts/perceptions) so a greater and wiser way can emerge. What if the way you see things due to your conditioning or experiences is lesser/smaller/lackluster compared to the greatness of your potential or ultimate purpose? Look at the events in your life that have revolutionized you and your mindset. Were these events fully in your awareness, or did you plot them? Or did they unfold, and you find yourself saying, "I could not have planned that or engineered that or see that coming or unfolding like that or conceive of that." The heart operates from love and the mind from a place of fear out of the need to protect us. Have you ever wanted something or a situation, and it ended up completely different but better than you expected? Make room for more of these beautiful moments in our lives. Let go of your own expectations or need to control the outcome so that a greater result or outcome can emerge. Allow more synchronicities to brighten the moments of life.

Coming home to yourself means choosing relationships based on the value you bring and how those relationships also pour into your soul.

I have had so many experiences of ending up empty over the years because I was not asking myself these questions:

"Is this relationship good for me?"

"Will this person pour into me as I pour into them?"

"I can add value to them, but will they also add value to me if it is in their power to do so?"

"Will they call my name in a room where I am not present and where opportunities are flowing?"

"Would they go the extra mile or do the same for me?"

I was so caught up with how I could help and simply help, but I realized this individualistic culture left me empty because people are conditioned to take, fill their cups, look out for what's in it for them, and move on. This is vital for people raised in collectivist cultures and romantic relationships.

For people from collectivist cultures, you have to look out for people raised in a culture that only looks out for self-gratification and not for how their actions and behaviors impact others. People from collective cultures are raised from birth to look out for others around them—how our actions or inactions impact the family and community at large. It is not so in the United States. This research regarding how American children's brain light up as if they were seeing a stranger when looking at a picture of their parents was shocking to me. Another reason why I am still searching for a 'home' is that collective selfishness in this culture can be quite harmful.

In romantic relationships, be sure to identify how your partner makes you feel, not how falling in love with them or being in love with them makes you feel. Make sure they are pouring into your cup, not just looking out for what you do for them.

Dear First-gen High-achieving Immigrant Woman

Be smart about the choices you are making in this individualistic culture. Be careful not to chase a career to the point where your personal life is sacrificed. Be mindful not to sacrifice your needs and desires for the needs of the family, community, or world. A person who lives a life solely in service to others can find all sorts of negative emotions because of this. Be intentional in balancing all of this with the beautiful opportunity to pursue your heart's desire in this country; I have noted so many women who chase careers and put off motherhood and other things that will water their gardens later in life until it is often too late. I see and hear of so many women who are having to go through fertility challenges because the 'doing world' took over their lives in their younger days.

I understand that finding a suitable mate in this culture can be both interesting and challenging, especially when you are often isolated and making these decisions on your own. It's important to surround yourself with people whose experienced eyes can see beyond your years and help you make the right choices. However, I urge you not to get carried away by the obsession with constant doing and neglect your connection to the essence of your being and your community.

If you're struggling to find balance in this doing culture, our coaching program can provide you with the necessary tools to create a more integrated and balanced lifestyle. Our *Thrive Abroad Coaching* program is focused on building on your strengths and applying cultural competency, which means we pay close attention to your culture of origin and how this impacts your way of thinking, operating, and worldview. Coming home to yourself, quieting the noisiness of the world we now live in, will reveal the answers you have long been searching externally for but were always right within reach, within you.

I understand the challenges faced as a first-generation immigrant, especially as a woman. Settling in a land of perceived abundance (although the developing world has its own abundance – don't underestimate it). I know the expectations of family, culture, communities back home, and the world. I know the hopes of so many that rest on you. I know that because you were born in a community and have eyes to see the hurts, the desires, the dreams, the fears, and more of those around you, it is not easy to disappear in this culture of individuality and forget your connectedness to everyone. Your superpower is that you can see not only your needs, desires, and hopes but also those of the people around you.

May God give you the wisdom to balance coming home to yourself and serving your family, the communities back home, and the world. Will you come home to rest, replenish, and tap into the treasures God has already placed in you?

You do not need another degree, certification, master's, PhD, or any other training.

You are enough.

You are already fully resourced.

If you are struggling under the weight of responsibility and duty to others. Do not get lost in the culture of doing. Do not lose who you are and your roots. America is the place where we immigrants come to forget who we are. Do not lose who you are, the wisdom from our families of origin, heritage, and communities of origin. We are stronger for integrating this new culture and our birth cultures of origin. We can absolutely accommodate, assimilate, and integrate both worlds to our advantage. You can choose the best of both worlds. Do not give up your superpower. Come home to yourself and entrust our coaching program to provide the support, insight, and foresight to help you create and integrate the immigrant life that you desire and deserve. Living with peace, joy, and purpose is possible, expressing the life God sent you here to live. Come home to yourself today. Your life, the lives of your loved ones, and your community depend on it. The world needs the healthy, fully resourced, aligned, whole version of you. You need and deserve to experience and behold the healthy, fully resourced, aligned, whole version of you. Do not lose another day giving up your power to this noisy, externally driven world. Come home to your voice and the gentle voice of your creator as clear and crisp as the breath you inhale and the early morning breeze against your skin. Coming home means to find the balance between both worlds and having a healthy self-image while serving community. It is essential to come home to yourself or risk being lost in this culture. On the other hand, you do not have to remain here. Have you ever thought of returning to the collectivist, your birth country, or somewhere else with more of a balance of being and doing?

Do you have psychological safety in this country and in this culture? Psychological safety means a condition in which a human being feels included and safe to learn, contribute, and challenge the status quo, all without fear of being embarrassed, marginalized, or punished in some way. Do you feel that here in the United States or any other adopted country where you currently reside? Know that you do have the power to move and find a place where you feel safe, supported, and free to become the person you have always known you could and deserve to become.

Don't forget who you are. Don't forget where you are from.

Do not forget your roots, heritage, and the shared wisdom in your former collectivist community. Don't forget your traditions.

There are so many voices here in this culture. Do you know how to recognize a fool? Just because someone attended an Ivy League university or came from a wealthy or affluent family does not mean that person has wisdom.

How do you recognize someone's underlying intentions and what drives or motivates them? Does any of their intentions support your self-interest? Do they mean you any good, or do they see you as a means to an end? Don't get eaten by the sharks in this culture. Many would have you believe there is no value in your birth country. That all that glitters here is gold but not all that is good for the goose is good for the gander.

Don't throw out the baby with the bath water. There is value in the old. There is wisdom in our ancestors. Some say that if people are not aware of their history, they will be lost or destined to repeat past mistakes. Don't forsake traditions or the former for the new. Tap into your superpower to have been one of the few to have lived in both a collectivist and an individualistic society. Tap into your superpower as a Third-Culture Hybrid (TCP). There are acres of diamonds if you slow down long enough to recognize both lessons. Nothing should be wasted.

CHAPTER 9

Just keep coming home to yourself,
you are the one who you've been waiting for.
— Byron Katie

The Benefits of Coming Home to Yourself

- **Coming home to yourself empowers** you to reset the system from other people's fears and beliefs and tap into your deeper inner wisdom.

- **Coming home to yourself means starting the journey of building the life you want**, no matter what chargeback messages you get from people who desire you to remain who you have always been.

- **Coming home to yourself means surrendering to your life's purpose.** This may look completely different from the one you have now. One that flows from a deeper connection with yourself rather than focused solely on the duty to family, community, and the world. It is possible to have a balanced, integrated life filled with the things, people, and circumstances that bring you joy organically.

- **Coming home to yourself means surrendering what you thought marriage should be** so that something greater can emerge. The culture in the individualistic world focuses on self-gratification at the expense of everything. Marriage can be a partnership between two people and a community (merging the collectivist and individualistic) built on trust, support, respect, and healthy boundaries. Coming home means shedding the corporate bitch, and things you have picked up since arriving in this world which do not serve you so you can come home to yourself, your spouse, your children, and the fullness/beauty of your feminine allure. Coming home for high-achieving immigrant women—how to make space for your spouse's wisdom and contributions to your marriage/relationships/union.

- **You do not have to do everything!** In fact, you can achieve more by doing less. Why do women do so much around the home and in a relationship? It's important to recognize that there is freedom when both partners create from a place of wholeness rather than from obligation and sacrifice. This allows for a balance of Yin and Yang. Maintaining your lifestyle before marriage and having children can be challenging. It's common to try to keep the same activity level despite taking on new responsibilities. As seasons change, one must let go of certain commitments to make room for what must happen during this new phase of life. It's also essential to release the external social pressure to "keep up with the Joneses."

- **Coming home means that you make space in your life to have the energy and awareness** to make healthier decisions that serve the sovereignty of who you are. You stop eating/doing things that do not serve you. Coming home means slowing down long enough to notice the messages your body and intuition have been trying to communicate but could not hear because of this advice-filled, noisy world. Coming home means that you allow yourself to tap into the wisdom and knowledge of the traditions and heritage from whence you come. Your body was designed to heal itself.

- **Coming home means slowing down for the day/moment to present itself, where you realize you are in control of your mind** and not the other way around. Use thinking to serve you, and do not let thinking or the conditioned mind control or use you.

- **Coming home means maturing into/returning to where you were when you arrived**—having a sense of worthiness rather than an everlasting sense of duty and cooperation with what everyone else thinks.

- **Coming home means that women stop waiting around for men.** Focusing externally on what they need to do to attract a certain man, but the magic happens when you fully accept who you are and come home to yourself. You will certainly attract someone who is vibrating energetically at the level you are if you are not operating from a place of wholeness. I have observed ladies in the church and elsewhere sitting around and sometimes wasting their lives waiting for a knight in shining armor to find them. It is as if their lives do not start until this event happens. Wake up, ladies! Come home to yourself and follow your deep longings for your soul/deeper self/divine purpose, and live fully. A relationship or marriage may not be a part of your journey. Can you accept that? Will you miss out on all that is possible for you by not coming home to yourself? Lost in the waiting for a man to bring you significance. Get up, move, dance, take a class, do something that brings you joy, something that motivates you out of bed. It is from that space of wholeness/fullness that you want to attract someone who mirrors that same level of wholeness into your life—not from a place of lack. Come home to yourself and see that even when the man arrives, he cannot make you happy unless you decide to choose your joy. Many women or men are unhappy because they feel that their spouses are responsible for making them happy. That could not be farther from the truth. Until you choose joy/tap into the joy already organically around you and within you, no one can convince you to choose that joy or live from that place of fullness. Joy is not outside of you, but rather, all can be found when you come home to yourself. Your spouse will not make you happy! You must choose happiness. No one holds that power but you. Happiness/joy is not a pursuit but can be found when you slow down, tune out the noise, and tune into the power within you from coming home to yourself. The joy, the happiness was within you all along. Come home to yourself. Slow down. Shut off the noise around you and the conditioning of the mind to allow what was there all along to come to the surface and emerge in your life. The person God originally intended you to be. Coming home means you do not pursue happiness or joy because it is already inside of you. You do not chase external things to find joy, peace, or moment-to-moment conditional happiness but rather look within for the spring that is already there—plugging back into the one God created within you.

- **Coming home means you become aware of codependent tendencies/ roles you play:** Letting/allowing life consequences to awaken people to their own power and agency. Coming home means you drop all those balls you carry that keep you from accomplishing God's will for your life, not the responsibility for everyone else's life. You are not responsible for everyone or for fixing everything. In fact, when you get out of the way, magic happens! When you get out of the way, divine wisdom enters and organically solves everything. Releasing the burden of feeling responsible for everyone and everything as a female.

Can you see something and not pick up or catch the ball? Can you see something and not feel obligated or have an internal drive that it is your responsibility to solve it, do it, care for it, fix it? You know you have come home to yourself when you can let go of all of this to create space for what was originally intended by God. If you are constantly fixing everybody and everything, these people often do not mature, grow up, learn from their own mistakes, and feel the impact of the consequences of their choices and behaviors. Do not be an enabler to people who are not maturing or growing up into what God intends for their lives. Free yourself! Your plate will get manageable, less stressed, less burdensome, more peaceful, and calmer in your soul. People will experience you in a whole new way—vibrant, light in spirit, joyful, and energetic. the person you were originally meant to be. Take lessons from nature. In fact, the resentment you feel melts away! Isn't it time you came home to yourself? There is freedom, and you just must choose it. Freedom for more inspired actions that can show up magically and truly what is needed for a particular moment. Many times, I made the wrong decisions in my dealings or under the guise that I needed to do something to help, but it turned out to be not so helpful or the best thing to have done, or people lied/took advantage of my kindness. When you come home to yourself - you create space for others to be themselves and not to conform to how you think they should be in your eyes but truly who they are without judgment.

Are you an immigrant savior? Do you operate from a place of survivor's guilt? Does it bother you that you are the one who made it out? You are the one who survived? You are the one who is in this land of abundance? Does this mentality serve you? Coming home to yourself will help you align with healthy boundaries to your duty to family, community, and the world. You do not have to sacrifice yourself or give everything to please the culture. There is and has always been space for your joy, peace, emotional health, rest, and more. Are you able to turn off that robotic human-doing who you have become? Giving feels so much better when your own cup is full and overflowing. As Iyanla Vanzant says, "What is in the cup is mine, and what flows out of the cup is for everyone."

If you feel burdened by guilt or shame because of your success and high-achieving nature, you may find that the people around you don't understand the challenges you face. They might assume that your life is easy. Our coaching program is designed to help you break free from these societal pressures and expectations. By prioritizing your mental, physical, and spiritual well-being, you can be kinder to yourself and to others. Our coaching will guide you in reconnecting with your true self, building self-control, and mastering your emotions, responses, reactions, and interactions with others. It is possible to stay true to a mature, healthy version of yourself. You have a better impact on your community, family, and friends when you are home to yourself. Not being tossed by the wind of everyone's ideas, everyone's perspectives, everyone's rightness for you but by aligning to the divine wisdom of God within. During the immigrant journey, it is possible to leave the collective to find the individual and then return on your terms to the collective after coming home to yourself. Coming home to yourself means that you give up the 'sacrifice' mentality of being the martyr.

How do you choose you? I remember the week before Mom declined. One Sunday evening, as we headed home after visiting, Mom said to me, "Simone, do not go." I responded, Mom, I have to go to work; our daughter has school tomorrow. How could I not have seen that would be the last time we would have a fully sober conversation with Mom? It was four days later that she declined, went to the emergency room, and never recovered. She returned home from the hospital on Christmas Day and departed on New Year's Day. I have since heard the story of another young lady who said the same exact scenario happened to her. As she visited her mom in the hospital, her mom asked her to stay with her and not to leave, but she had to work and missed saying farewell to her mom. How much do we have to sacrifice in this culture of doing? Is it showing up to work at the expense of our loved one's worth it? This was a hard lesson to swallow. I tear up every time I reminisce. As immigrants, we get lost in the duty to work and support other people's ventures, and we often cannot choose ourselves and our family when it is most essential.

- Coming home means changing your environment if it doesn't allow you to be your authentic self. Not the other way around. Stop the shapeshifting. I have watched people around who sacrifice who they are to fit in the demands of an office environment or social scene to feel accepted. They changed at the core. Over the years, in different work environments, I would struggle with becoming what I saw people changing into, and it was like I was stuck in indecision. Oftentimes, I was able to leave and choose myself, but this is not always the case for many who are bound by the responsibility to provide.

- Coming home means giving yourself the grace to fail and recover fast to learn the lessons from each missing mark. Talking about your failures without shame because that is where the gold is. The diamonds are in the lessons, the experiences, and the angles of perspectives you have gained.

Coming home allows you to change your relationship with failure or missing the proverbial mark. Failure is not in the cards as first-gen immigrants and children of immigrants. This can bring so much emotional pressure and could keep us stuck in inaction. Coming home to yourself welcomes the idea that sometimes you win and sometimes you lose some. Life is not perfect. Perfection will cause us to get stuck and unable to move because of the fear of failure. It is important to allow yourself to miss the mark as many times as possible, so you learn to recover fast and not simmer in sadness, guilt, or shame. Giving grace to yourself first replaces fear as you come home to yourself. There is no need to fear making mistakes because we never lose in taking action. We learn, gain clarity, get information about what we do not want, and get closer to being aligned with our purpose if we take the time to reflect and learn the lessons. In fact, all things are working together for your highest good. Come home and surrender to your divine purpose.

Come home and create space for your authentic self to emerge and shine through. Ladies, our young girls and others are watching what you do, not what you say. They see how you recover from missing the mark, constantly moving the target as soon as you arrive at an accomplishment in this capitalistic shapeshifting culture where desire is never quenched. If you do decide to change, it should be on your terms from coming home to yourself. Coming home to yourself means that you can sooner begin to live out and pursue the purpose you are here on this earth to live out. Don't let us miss out on the power, peace, beauty, and flow that comes from someone operating indignantly, unapologetically, and fully from being tuned into the divine purpose for your being here. It's your obligation to come home to yourself. It's your obligation to the world to live from that place of awareness and connection. Do not rob us of experiencing what you are meant to teach us.

> *What is in the cup is mine*
> *but what flows out of the cup is for others*
> —Iyanla Vanzant

- Coming home means finding the voice you always had as a child when you were so sure of yourself. Message to immigrant parents: Please do not talk your child out of their voice. Sons raised by women are young adults without their voice and identity.

- Coming home means no longer allowing others to drain your energy and time. This is about my experience working with coaches: a business coach who never delivered, a brand coach who gaslighted me, and a coach with whom I did not feel aligned.

- Coming home means rediscovering myself after shedding responsibility and roles that no longer serve me. It means balancing the desire for togetherness with solitude.

- Coming home means tapping into the wholeness already within so that you can be a healthy partner. What are the expectations of our partners in marriages and friendships? They should not prevent us from truly experiencing the essence of the people in our lives. The 'shoulds' block the authentic person.

- Religion and Coming Home to Yourself. The impact of Religious Doctrine on everyday life: Research around humility, sacrifice, and service. People who completely neglect themselves to serve others. Coming home to yourself helps create a healthier balance. Finding oneself through giving yourself away in service - it's in coming home to yourself and having self-compassion that one can give fully. Collectivist cultures and how unhealthy it can be to overlook the individual to serve the collective. Individualistic culture and the what's in it for me mindset ensures that givers are left with empty cups because of all the takers in this culture.

- Individualistic vs. collectivist: the good, bad, and ugly. Taking the meat and leaving the bones. Coming home means answering the question, "Who are you uninterrupted? What are you like uninterrupted?"

- Coming home means working harder on yourself than you do at any place of employment. Know your why. Once you discover your why, you will be unstoppable. Concept of money and why it is called currency. Mimics the flow of energy and life. People go after money, but their lives do not reflect abundance, so they don't keep it or keep the flow. Jim Rohn - work harder on yourself and develop yourself more than you do on any job. Money will have no choice but to find you or flow to you when you get your inner world right. Jim Rohn - "Income seldom exceeds personal development." Coming home means learning what drives you, your insecurities, your family of origin, guilt, shame, or other things. Coming home means not letting other people's labels define you. Coming to yourself means exploring and being aware of your needs and being selective in relationships and other actions to ensure that your personal needs and garden are being watered.

- Coming home means ensuring your cup is always full and your energy is replenished. If people are drinking from your well, make sure you are receiving to keep your well replenished.

- Coming home to yourself means that when the challenges and pressures come, we pull out the drawers that God has placed in us to find the treasures that God originally equipped us with. You are fully resourced. You are enough as you are. You are sufficient. You do not need another degree, another master's, or a PhD.

CHAPTER 10

Don't stress the could haves;
if it should have, it would have
—Unknown

Stop 'Should-ing' on Yourself

For most of my time on this earth, I have been ruled by other people's shoulds. I should be a good daughter. I should be a good student. I should respect adults, even the abusive ones. I should go to college, get good grades, do well, make my family proud, look good, and not do anything to embarrass or shame them. I should be a good Christian girl. I should not get pregnant too early. I should follow what the church says even though it did not make logical sense or people's behaviors in the church played out another reality. I should find a good Christian guy to marry and then start our family. He should be this tall, have this level of education, look like this, come from this background, and be able to provide for our family fully. I should be a stay-at-home Mom. We should behave this way in marriage. Marriage should look this way. A wife should do this. A husband should do that. Should on top of more shoulds. All I know is that it is time to shed these shoulds of others to allow for real, authentic living.

Be Here Now

Life is what happens now; however, it is unfolding for you—not someone else's journey or experience but yours. Can you shut out the noise of your indoctrinated/conditioned mind and external influences to align with what is happening/flowing through you NOW? We are vessels of the divine creator, not conditioned personalities. Not what the Joneses or the Kardashians or other celebrities or neighbors or other friends and family members are doing but your present moment—your gift of life as an individual. I did not realize how much this ruled my actions, thinking, and decisions until shortly after 2022. Can you imagine being unwell but still feeling urges or being pulled by responsibilities? You did not choose obligations to people you hardly know or understand, so why should you continue these obligations? These urges left me with sleepless nights, emotional unsettledness, and an overall feeling of disorientation that is unexplainable. This is the reality of many first-generation immigrants and children of immigrant parents (I would imagine this is similar for many others, too) living in a land that flows with milk and honey. I had had enough. It suddenly occurred to me that I was living a life full of indoctrination and conditioning by others. It only took me going through another phase of burnout to realize this. Wait, why am I doing this? Why do these urges and obligations control me? Whose 'shoulds' are these? Who am I pleasing by doing this? Oh yeah, they will approve of me. They will not shame or guilt me if I do this or continue these outdated obligations. This will make so and so happy. This person will be pleased with me. Then, this thought, which had surfaced at different times over the years, came up again.

What do you desire, Simone?

Are you doing what you are here to do or expressing your authentic essence?

I have spent most of my adult life following a script that people around me say is the ideal, the expectation, the pleasing way to live my life. I have swallowed my own voice to choose the responsible thing to do, the thing to do because it will help the next person coming behind me. Is it possible to listen to that gentle, quiet voice to the full extent?

If not now, then when?

I had followed all the 'shoulds' of others and did the responsible things, but it left me sad inside and unable to get out of bed on many days. How is it possible that I have achieved or am living the life that many females would covet and not be simply joyful and happy? Isn't this what I thought I wanted? Isn't this what I should have done? Didn't I do what was expected of me as a good child? I had the master's degree, the career, the husband, the child, the home in a posh part of town, the private school education, and taking tennis and golf lessons. What more could I want or should have done? I was feeling empty. None of this filled me up. The treadmill came to a screeching halt. I had forced myself to keep going because it was the responsible thing to do. I could no longer continue this way:

- forcing myself to show up despite being sick.
- forcing myself to give—even when the budget did not support it.
- forcing myself to give up by using debt using credit even when my education and knowledge knew better.
- forcing myself to get on another work-travel job assignment despite the exhaustion and numbness.

I had to keep going because people were depending on me. You know what? No one even knew my darkest moments. These same people had no idea what struggles I faced. These people did not know (and it felt at times like they didn't care) of the pain I felt inside. Real or perceived, they only wanted to keep the support coming. How difficult could it be? You have this great career and life; what challenges could you possibly face because all they could see was the outward?

Remember to Keep Wearing your Oxygen Mask

It was 2022, and I realized that no one was coming to save me. I had to save myself. I was in the midst of a challenging situation at work, and the flashbacks flooded my mind. *Simone, you keep ignoring that still, small voice - your intuition and its guidance.* This same situation had happened once before at work. I was repeating the same cycle. Wait, how did I get here again? Focusing on what was solely required of me for work and living solely from a place of duty and responsibility in my life left me with feelings of guilt. This one needs help. That one needs help. You have to be an example for those around you and those coming behind. You must pull up and help up as you climb. I was always distracted by other people's stuff, and it felt impossible to just do me. I've often wondered how much more successful I might have been if I had focused on what I needed to do for my career and life. I am not saying that I would not give and help as needed, but the cultural expectations of immigrants can be debilitating. Serving others and giving can be done when the home is taken care of, and one is not bleeding. My plate was always overflowing. The feelings of guilt and shame from those around me when they were displeased that I was only doing me came rushing in. When does this stop? Is it not enough that I am doing the darnedest to stay out of trouble, to not shame my parents, family, and community, not doing drugs, sleeping around, and all the things parents worry and fear that their children will do as they grow older?

All the times I had ignored, the still, small voice flooding my memory and how things did not work in my favor for ignoring the warnings, the caution, the are you sure moments. My life seems to hit a crisis moment or change almost every five to seven years. I was in the midst of another. No one saved me the last time. No one was coming to save me this time either. I waited. No one came. I had to pull up my big girl panties and dig myself out of this hole I had once again fallen in by ignoring that still, small voice and not focusing on my plate but distracted by the plate of others. The funniest thing is that these people were not going around being concerned about how I was faring and whether I needed assistance. None of them called just to check on me, only when they needed something.

When will you start listening to your deeper self-guidance, Simone, and stop doing things out of responsibility, duty, and the desire to please others? The emptiness inside screamed even louder. It is now or never. So, I started reflecting. I started looking around at the people who came to take and who would be considered in my inner circle and realized they were only feeding from my well and that they could not replenish or water my well.

I cried. I got angry. I went silent.

How could I have neglected myself this way? It was never about what was important or what Simone needed but how does this serve the greater whole or the collective. Wow, did someone do a number on me!

I started saying no. I did not know the level of fear inside of me at the thought of simply saying this two-letter word to everything, which did not make space for me. I started saying no to things to make space for Simone.

What would life be like if I, for once, gave full attention to my intuition, my guidance system, and my joy?

What would life look like uninterrupted?

What is Simone like when she's uninterrupted?

The passing of my mother made me realize that tomorrow is never guaranteed. Did I want to leave this earth without accomplishing what the creator had for me to do? It's a struggle to balance supporting the collective and integrating our own desires. I see other first-generation immigrant women and men going through the same thing. They feel so externally controlled that they have no time for themselves. For instance, a single mother who fears saying no to friends who have helped her in the past, even when her health, home, and immediate family need her to 'come home to herself.' Heck, I needed to come home to my daughter. Life would likely feel calmer and easily flow if I re-aligned my priorities.

I live in an individualistic society, trying to maintain collective values, which only makes me feel empty. The struggle to balance the expectations of the collective while only having a limited amount of energy, time, and resources to accomplish the successes in an individualistic society to even be able to be altruistic in a healthy way is real. There is always another person in need. As working parents, we do everything. There is no community help like back home. The line does not seem to end. I had to decide who I would become. Continuing this cycle, I see so many struggling with the TCP hybrid of integrating and balancing both cultures. I had to choose and design a life that reflected a new integration of something else, something healthier.

Business, as usual, just was not serving me.

Business as usual could not continue as is.

This type of disorientation is unexplainable at times unless you are walking through it. Changing some of these behaviors, acknowledging them, and finding the words to decipher the emotions, the sadness, and the emptiness can feel insurmountable. This may explain why I have reverted to the old behaviors in the past, simply because it was easier to let the past messages control me. I know one thing: I had to stop giving up my power; I had to take full responsibility for the next season of my life. I could not continue blaming external circumstances and/or people for my burnout. I have to come home to myself. My daughter, my husband, my life, and a healthy home depended on it.

An interesting dynamic can happen in collectivist settings where some in the group are natural givers and others organic takers. The takers never take on the responsibility to the collective. This becomes interesting for a collective as the group moves into an individualistic society where everyone has the freedom to be selfish. The givers must make intentional behavioral changes to ensure their needs are met. It becomes even more pronounced in the WIIFM individualistic culture. Being in the WIIFM culture can make one feel like he or she is being used or taken advantage of as this group does not give back. They come, fill their tank, and keep it moving. This can get dangerous for a giver from a collectivist background who innately looks out for the group. Look around; you will see them in your church, school, home, and elsewhere. I have felt this way many times: being so focused on the needs of the needy that I neglected important relationships—the people who were pouring into me. I had to stop and say no to the leakage so that I could bless those who were blessing me. However, it's important to maintain a balance in your relationships, ensuring that those relationships that nurture you are being nurtured—this is part of caring for yourself. The thing is that the takers likely cannot, will not, and do not have it to pour back into you. This was a difficult lesson for me to learn. I realized that I had neglected the people who were nurturing and supporting me, as I was too focused on meeting the needs of others.

I was an immigrant-savior suffering from immigrant survivor's guilt. After helping a few people, I clearly remember thinking to myself, who is next? Coming from a large family, the line never ended. There was always someone else in the line needing to be helped. I felt exhausted just thinking about it. This fed into codependent tendencies. There was always another person who needed saving. It was amazing how much this occupied my thinking.

In 2023, I embarked on a journey of self-discovery to find and follow my joy and align with my soul's purpose. Whenever I felt obligated to do something, I would pause, reflect, and decide whether I wanted to continue with that behavior. The truth is that many of these behaviors had so many discomforts and emotions tied to them. I had been ignoring them because I was so busy over the past two decades, constantly moving, changing relationships, switching jobs, chasing the next best role, and rescuing one person after the other. I remember one guy saying I carried a motherly presence a few years back, which unsettled me. I was not yet a mother, and this puzzled me. I would go around looking for the next person's issues to champion, support, and rescue – I now know that is the Clifton Strengths Maximizer trait and can now use it in a healthy way. That is why it is so vital to know yourself. Did I get this from being the eldest child? Was this from the collectivist cultural dynamic? Still unclear, but this behavior was deeply embedded within me. The funny thing is that it showed up in rescuing, which led to me neglecting important relationships and myself—there was always someone else bleeding around me. I had given my power away in so many ways.

I can definitely relate to feeling like a puppet being controlled at times in my life. It's a difficult feeling to shake off. The key to taking control of our decisions is to start by recognizing that we can say no without feeling guilty or ashamed. We have the right to prioritize our needs and desires without worrying about pleasing others. Of course, it is easier said than done, but I believe that with practice, we can learn to shift our focus from pleasing the collective to pleasing ourselves. It is all about taking small steps, working those muscles, and being patient with ourselves along the way. We have to shut out the noise:

- Turn off the phone.
- Stop calling. Stop taking calls.
- Saying no.
- Let go of relationships that only take from us.
- Make space for the new to come alive within us.

CHAPTER 11

Keep your language.
Love its sounds, its modulation, its rhythm.
But try to march together with men of different languages,
remote from your own, who wish like you for a more
just and human world.
—Hélder Câmara

Navigating Identity: The Immigrant's Journey of Cultural Integration and Balance

Who are you becoming? Are you becoming American? Are you becoming a collectivist or individualistic? Are you becoming a hybrid of your birth and adopted country? Are you becoming the balanced, savvy, integrated immigrant? Is it possible to still respect the former and make space for the new? Is it possible to have the best of both worlds, where you have a healthy relationship dynamic with yourself and the people from the collective culture but can live freely without shame and/or guilt in pursuing your own desires? How do you balance being a 'human-doing' and the human being? How do you strike a healthy balance—navigating the tension between collectivist cohesion and individualistic independence?

Collectivist and individualistic cultures represent different cultural orientations that influence how individuals within society interact with others and perceive their roles within the community. These orientations impact various aspects of life, including social relationships, decision-making, values, and priorities.

Here are the main traits associated with collectivist and individualistic cultures:

Collectivist Cultures:

- Group Harmony and Unity: Emphasis on maintaining social harmony and unity within the community.
- Prioritization of the needs and goals of the group over individual desires.

- Interdependence and Cooperation: Value interdependence and cooperation, often emphasizing collaboration and collective effort.
- Strong sense of responsibility towards the family, extended family, and community.
- Family and Community Focus: Close-knit family structures are highly valued. Family's needs and opinions often supersede individual aspirations.
- Collective Decision-making: Decisions are often made collectively, considering the input and opinions of family members or the community. Collective consensus and consultation are significant in decision-making processes.
- Group Identity and Loyalty: Strong identification with a particular group, such as family, clan, or community. Loyalty to the group and its well-being is prioritized.
- Interpersonal Relationships: Strong interpersonal relationships are highly valued. Relationship bonds often extend beyond immediate family to include extended family, neighbors, and community members.
- Modesty and Humility: Modesty is valued, and individuals are encouraged to downplay personal achievements. Public recognition is often seen as inappropriate or boastful.

Individualistic Cultures:
- Personal Autonomy and Independence: Emphasis on personal autonomy, self-expression, and individual rights. Priority given to personal goals, aspirations, and self-fulfillment.
- Competitiveness and Self-Reliance: Encouragement of competition and self-reliance. Individuals often compete for opportunities and success in various domains.
- Nuclear Family Emphasis: The nuclear family (parents and children) is more heavily emphasized than the extended family. Individual needs and goals often precede the larger community's needs.
- Individual Decision-making: Decisions are often made independently or with minimal consultation. Personal opinions and preferences carry significant weight in decision-making.
- Personal Achievement and Recognition: Emphasis on personal achievements and recognition for one's accomplishments. Individual recognition and public acknowledgment are valued and encouraged.

- Direct Communication Style: Direct and explicit communication is often preferred, expressing one's opinions and desires clearly. Open expression of thoughts and feelings is encouraged.

- Personal Responsibility: There is a strong emphasis on personal responsibility for one's actions and decisions. Individuals are accountable for their own success, well-being, and development.

As I came across the clear-cut definitions of the collectivist vs individualistic culture, I thought—if I only had this clear understanding at the start of my immigrant journey, I would have saved myself so many days, months, and years of disorientation and confusion trying to make sense of my emotions, actions, inactions and that of others. I am becoming American. Recently, a friend said, "You are very American in your worldview." What? I did not see that coming because I tend to still feel like an outsider with many everyday Americans. [Though, one high school friend expressed just how much I had changed from being Jamaican. This, I take with a grain of salt because this person has never left the island much in over 25 years and likely had not changed much living in the same cultural dynamic. I would like to see if this person could remain the same after living in a foreign culture for 25 years or more].

I like basketball and football and can sit through a baseball game at the stadium, but I am not a fanatic to the point that many Americans express their love. I still do not like bar hopping. I would rather be at home and enjoy long conversations around a firepit roasting, going to the beach, hiking, or spending time at a cabin. I was raised in the countryside, and nature interweaves into my soul. Nevertheless, I did most of my adult education in the U.S., mixed in with international work and travel, which explains my worldview.

Our family has this running joke when we see certain expressions, "That's that Jamaican in her," I have coined the opposite, "That's that American in me." How do you know when you have changed from your birth culture to your adopted culture? I see it in my cooking. I cannot remember anyone cooking with parsley in our family, but I am now in love with parsley in my sauteed vegetables. I now use squash instead of only cucumbers. I now use turmeric instead of straight Jamaican curry. I have had to find substitutes for the items we are used to eating in this new world. There was no way around it. I found that I would eat junk or highly processed foods, which only turned out to be extremely harmful if I did not plan my meals to find healthy substitutes.

In what ways have you changed?

Do you feel like you have become a foreigner in the place you once called home?

Do you fit in when you return to your original home?

Do you fit in the U.S., or do you have to find other third-culture bridge people?

It is important to make sense of the change in us. Are you becoming more American or holding on to the old culture for dear life? I have found that beginning these kinds of conversations via our podcast, The Immigrant Experience in America, has helped me understand the experience of disorientation. I have grown, gained insight, and broadened my perspective, empathy, and worldview. How are you making sense of the internal battle? What has been your experience as you changed from your birth culture to that of your adopted country? Do you even have the language to talk about it? Are you still unable to explain the emotions you are having? Join our community of third-culture bridge people as we help each other make sense of the new world and who we are becoming.

In a world where workplaces often reflect the dominant cultural norms, many individuals from marginalized backgrounds find themselves struggling to fit into spaces that were never designed with them in mind. The pressure to meet standards that do not account for diverse identities can be crushing, leading to feelings of doubt and uncertainty. It is not just about personal insecurities; it is about a system that continuously sidelines those who do not fit the traditional mold. When the rules of professionalism are written by and for a narrow group, it is no wonder that so many talented people feel like they do not belong. However, the problem isn't with them—it is with the biases that pervade our institutions and the exclusionary practices that keep them in place.

(a) Bias and Exclusion Exacerbate Feelings of Doubt

Many individuals are often told, either directly or indirectly, that they do not belong in workplaces that White males dominate. This is because the assessment process for determining who is considered 'professional' is culturally biased and skewed, as noted by Tina Opie, an associate professor at Babson College. When employees from marginalized backgrounds attempt to meet a standard that no one like them has met before (and that they are not typically expected to meet), the pressure to excel can become overwhelming. For example, a Latina woman who was once engaged in her work may suddenly become quiet in meetings. In contrast, an Indian woman who was a strong candidate for promotion may receive vague feedback about lacking leadership presence. A trans woman who previously spoke up may stop doing so after being subjected to gender-insensitive remarks by her manager, and a Black woman who once provided valuable feedback may no longer feel comfortable doing so after being told that she is not a team player.

Unfortunately, women of color face even greater feelings of doubt due to their chronic battles with systemic bias and racism. In truth, we do not belong because we were never supposed to belong. Our presence in most of these spaces results from decades of grassroots activism and begrudgingly developed legislation. Academic institutions and corporations are still mired in the cultural inertia of the "good ole' boys" clubs and White supremacy. Biased practices across institutions routinely hinder the ability of individuals from underrepresented groups to truly thrive. The answer to overcoming the imposter phenomenon is not to fix individuals but to create an environment that fosters a variety of leadership styles in which diverse racial, ethnic, and gender identities are seen as just as professional as the current model, which Opie describes as usually "Eurocentric, masculine, and heteronormative."

According to organizational psychologist Tomas Chamorro-Premuzic: "The truth is that pretty much anywhere in the world, men tend to think that they are much smarter than women. However, arrogance and overconfidence are inversely related to leadership talent—the ability to build and maintain high-performing teams and to inspire followers to set aside their selfish agendas to work for the group's common interest." The same systems that reward confidence in male leaders, even if they are incompetent, punish White women for lacking confidence, women of color for showing too much of it, and all women for demonstrating it in a way that's deemed unacceptable. These biases are insidious and complex and stem from narrow definitions of acceptable behavior drawn from White male models of leadership. Research from Kecia M. Thomas finds that too often, women of color enter their companies as pets but are treated as threats once they gain influence in their roles. Women of color are by no means a monolith, but we are often linked by our common experiences of navigating stereotypes that hold us back from reaching our full potential.

It is time to stop telling women and marginalized groups that they need to change—and start changing the environments that hold them back.

(b) Fixing Bias, Not Women

Imposter syndrome refers to the feeling of inadequacy and fraudulence that people experience, often leading them to believe they do not deserve success. This phenomenon is particularly prevalent in cultures that value individualism and overwork, which can be toxic and biased towards women. However, the idea of "fixing women's imposter syndrome" has persisted for decades despite its flaws. Instead of trying to fix this issue, we need to focus on creating inclusive workplaces that foster a sense of belonging and allow marginalized professionals to thrive. This requires a cultural shift at a broader level. Leaders must create a culture for women and people of color that addresses systemic bias and racism. Only by doing so can we reduce the experiences that culminate in so-called imposter syndrome among employees from marginalized communities—or at the very least, help those employees channel healthy self-doubt into positive motivation, which is best fostered within a supportive work culture. Perhaps then we can stop misdiagnosing women with "imposter syndrome" once and for all (Harvard Business Review). When a plant loses luster and begins to shrivel up, we put it in the sunlight and add water and new soil to nourish it to grow and return to its former brilliance. The same applies to immigrants, BIPOC, and other untapped groups of people; we do not change who we are, only the environments in which we have to exist.

Personal and Professional Barriers

Research on skilled immigrants who bring valuable cultural and professional skills to their adopted countries but are unable to utilize those skills highlights several key themes and issues:

1. Credential Recognition and Employment Barriers

One of the primary challenges skilled immigrants face is the non-recognition of their foreign qualifications and credentials. Many countries have stringent processes for recognizing foreign degrees and professional licenses, which often results in skilled immigrants being underemployed or working in jobs that do not match their qualifications.

- Credential Recognition Issues: Studies have shown that immigrants with foreign credentials often face lengthy and costly processes to have their qualifications recognized. For example, a study by the Migration Policy Institute found that many skilled immigrants in the U.S. and Canada struggle with credential recognition, which hampers their ability to find employment in their field.

- Employment Barriers: According to the OECD, skilled immigrants often face employment barriers such as lack of local work experience, language proficiency issues, and discrimination. These barriers prevent them from accessing jobs commensurate with their skills and experience.

2. Economic Impact of Underemployment

Underemployment of skilled immigrants has significant economic implications for individuals and the host country. When skilled immigrants cannot work in their field, it represents a loss of human capital and potential economic growth.

- Loss of Human Capital: The under-utilization of skilled immigrants' talents can lead to brain waste, where the skills and knowledge of highly educated individuals are not fully utilized. This results in a significant economic loss for the host country.

- Economic Integration: Research by the Institute for the Study of Labor (IZA) found that better integration of skilled immigrants into the labor market could substantially increase the economic contributions of immigrants, boosting productivity and innovation.

3. Social and Psychological Impact

The inability to use their skills in the adopted country can also have adverse social and psychological effects on skilled immigrants.

- Identity and Self-Esteem: The mismatch between their qualifications and the jobs they end up doing can lead to a loss of professional identity and lower self-esteem. This can affect their overall well-being and mental health.

- Social Integration: Skilled immigrants who cannot find appropriate employment may also struggle with social integration, feeling isolated and marginalized within the host society.

4. Strategies for Improvement

Research suggests several strategies to integrate skilled immigrants into the labor market better and utilize their skills effectively:

- Streamlined Credential Recognition: Simplifying and expediting the process for recognizing foreign qualifications can help skilled immigrants enter the labor market more quickly.

- Bridging Programs: Offering programs that bridge the gap between foreign and local qualifications, such as additional training or certification courses, can be beneficial.

- Employer Engagement: Encouraging employers to recognize and value foreign credentials and work experience can help skilled immigrants find jobs that match their qualifications.

- Support Services: Providing language training, mentorship programs, and other support services can assist skilled immigrants in overcoming barriers to employment.

Skilled immigrants bring valuable cultural and professional skills to their adopted countries, but various barriers often prevent them from fully utilizing these skills. Addressing credential recognition, employment barriers, and social integration issues is crucial for maximizing the potential of skilled immigrants and ensuring their successful integration into the labor market.

Listen to episodes 156-158 for the story of the spouse of an H1B and the challenges she encountered finding meaningful work. The struggles can be debilitating.

Immigration is a life change generally made to improve one's overall quality of life and well-being while increasing the risk of challenges that can impact mental health and overall well-being. According to most literature on immigrant mental health, successful adaptation to the host country, including overcoming occupation, language, and other barriers, is an essential part of the immigration process (Delara, 2016). Issues immigrants often encounter that can impact their overall well-being include discrimination, societal prejudices, occupation changes, migratory grief and loss, and language and education barriers (Aroian et al., 2003). Burnout and secondary traumatic stress are risks for mental health professionals due to the nature and demands of their work (O'Connor et al., 2018). Thus, for mental health professionals who are immigrants, there may be an escalated risk of burnout and trauma.

Heavily influenced by the micro,[4] meso,[5] and exo[6] systems, the immigration process contributes to profound losses and disruptions in identity (Berger et al., 2004). The result is the loss of the cultural self and the need to reconstruct a self that integrates the original culture while meeting the demands of the new macro system (Martínez Rosas, 2020). Kuo (1976) and Espin (1987) were the first researchers to claim a relationship between migration experiences and potential psychological distress. They described migratory grief as the consequence of immigration,

---

4   Micro system: the direct environment we have in our lives, including our family, friends, classmates, teachers, neighbors, and other people who have direct contact with us.

5   Meso system: involves the relationships between the microsystems in one's life. This means that your family experience may be related to your school experience.

6   Exo system: includes external environmental factors that indirectly influence an individual's development, such as parental workplace policies and mass media.

relocation, and resettlement, which are the disconnection of both the symbolic and physical self. This disconnection in self can result from separation from the old exosystem, including but not limited to the climate, food, community, laws, and practices (Espin, 1987; Kuo, 1976). In essence, it's an individual reaction to variables that trigger changes across systems that influence one's thoughts, feelings, and behaviors.

Barreto (2013) found that immigrant psychotherapists who work in the United States deal with culture shock and a sense of belonging nowhere, which leads to multiple stressors that can contribute to feelings of vulnerability surrounding their professional identity.

There were similar findings in Kissil et al. (2013) study of immigrant therapists' acculturation and counseling self-efficacy. Results demonstrated that the more acculturated the immigrant therapist described being, the higher they perceived their self-efficacy. However, this may come at a cost. A study with immigrant students in counselor education found that while acculturation of Euro-normative behaviors helped participants navigate their professional identity, they felt that to be their culturally authentic selves, they had to hide their heritage, culture, values, and behaviors (Interiano & Lim, 2018).

5. Social Support

The following vignettes offer a broad perspective and insights into the inevitable burnout that high-achieving women face in every aspect of their lives:

In her blog, Betsy Jordyn says, "I had not realized I was suffering from burnout. I only noticed that I became unmotivated to accomplish anything. Everything seemed like a never-ending workout. I became enraged with myself because I was never able to meet my high expectations because I was emotionally exhausted. My mother's drive to succeed and prosper lived through me."

Various other women's perspectives include:

1. Unlike men, who are wired to be single and focused on a specific result, women are wired to notice everything. Alison Armstrong calls it "diffuse awareness." Women pay attention to the work at hand, all the emotions, needs, and concerns of the people we work with, how our home looks, and what is going on with our friends. And if we have children…you can only imagine what our "Mommy brain" does to that challenge!

2. Women are wired to be pleasers not because we are weak but because it is a part of our survival instinct. Striving to be perfect and pleasing is a way to ensure we have a place in a protective group, similar to how lionesses hunt together. Our biological need to be pleasing often leads to prioritizing others' needs over our own, leading to burnout. The solution to this is not for high-achieving women to do less, but rather to prioritize self-care and recharge their personal energy. This includes learning to say "no," delegating tasks more effectively and organizing activities that recharge our batteries. It also involves letting go of the need for perfection and accepting "good enough." Let go of the illusion of the perfect person—that fake ideal woman who can run a company and raise her kids without any help. She doesn't exist.

Strategies to cope:

- It is possible to enjoy life with reduced anxiety.
- Being kind to yourself and having compassion is essential.
- Boundaries are essential to maintain mental and emotional health.
- Being in control of yourself is achievable, and you have choices.
- Learn how to make yourself a priority.

Quiet that negative self-talk and replace it with kindness and self-compassion:

- Get back in control of yourself by making healthier choices.
- Discover that whole 'work-life balance/integration' thing.
- Feel confident you have the tools to relax and calm your mind and body.

As you reflect on the complexities of navigating life between cultures, remember that your journey is uniquely yours. The process of becoming—whether more American, more connected to your roots, or a blend of both—is not about choosing sides but about embracing the fluidity of your identity. It is about finding harmony in the tension between collectivist cohesion and individualistic independence and creating a life that honors your past while making space for your future. Ultimately, the goal is not just to integrate but to thrive, crafting a balanced, authentic self that can move confidently between worlds. As you continue this journey, know that you are not alone—there is a community of others who, like you, are learning to blend, bridge, and build a life that respects where they come from and where they are headed.

CHAPTER 12

We need resources to combat stress
and prevent distress.
And we need mechanisms to manage
our reactions to being triggered.

– Faith Harper

Coming Home to Yourself and Coping Mechanisms

What are you like uninterrupted? Uninterrupted by the voices of those around, though well-meaning. Are you hungry for a version of yourself that is still unknown? The version stifled by the 'shoulds,' of the cultural expectations?

When will you come home to yourself?

When will you make space for you?

Is there a world where you are not weighed down by responsibility and duty? I know this might sound like developed world problems, but if you are living outside the so-called developed world, cherish your quiet moments of solitude and connectedness. The hustle and bustle of life across the seas may not be all that is being sold to you, as projected from all the different screens you watch. Are you one of those who daydream of getting across the seas to somewhere else, anywhere else but where you are? Know that life is not always what you see on the screens.

Can you, too, come home to yourself and find joy, gratitude, peace, and abundance right where you are?

Can you find fulfillment if you never make it to the developed world to study, work, or go on an excursion? Take it from us: life in the industrial, developed world is not for the faint of heart. Many work to pay bills and send money back home. Will you be okay with that? Many work until they are dead.

What does it look like if you began to go against the grain of those roles you play in the collective? Does your soul yearn for a reality and experience that is starkly different from the one you know? The one where you had no say in what you are born into, the expectation that you are born into? Have you ever allowed the thought to rest within you, or are you still running away from it? These shadows will not disappear or fade but will continue to influence you. Can you wake up to the idea that the world will experience you differently when you show up as your authentic self? You will experience yourself wholly different from the exhausted, burnt-out, restless person you are today.

It is possible to have a balanced, integrated immigrant life. One where you come alive from being aligned with your divine purpose and live daily with joy, peace, and intentionality. One where you attract success rather than chasing success. One where you come home to yourself and allow the divine to flow, synchronize, and direct you. Have you ever wondered what it would be like if things went well with you? You are uniquely positioned for such a time as this, born in the collective society, matured in the individualistic world, to choose a healthier way of showing up.

Will you come home to yourself today?

As one who has intimately traveled the road of a person born in a collectivist culture and transitioning to an individualistic culture, the journey of coming home to oneself is not an easy undertaking. However, it can be done with the appropriate support, knowledge, and cultural competence, such as our *Thriving Abroad* coaching program.

A journey of a thousand miles begins with small steps. Small steps toward affirming yourself, finding your voice, and creating space for the best version of you to emerge and thrive.

Here are some steps I took to come home to myself:

Living in the United States offers the privilege of being surrounded by abundant information at our fingertips. However, the challenge lies in deciphering what is relevant and identifying unreliable sources. It's unsettling to think that data can be manipulated to support false or harmful ideas and even more unsettling that it can be publicly released, making it difficult to distinguish between truth and falsehood. We have to fact-check the information we encounter online on a daily basis, as we can no longer rely solely on trusted sources for information.

It took me a while to understand the concept of self-interest and its importance. I first learned about this in an undergrad class, and I was confused for years about how to prioritize my own needs and desires. In a collective society, there's nothing wrong with prioritizing the group, but in an individualistic world, it's crucial to consider your own self-interest regularly. Otherwise, you could get taken advantage of in a competitive environment where everyone is looking out for themselves. This is especially important for immigrants, as you'll need to interact with various organizations and businesses that are focused on their own self-interest. It took me a long time to realize this and adapt to this individualistic mindset, as I was initially steeped in a collective way of thinking. While making a community impact is important, it shouldn't come at the expense of neglecting your own needs and being lost in a culture that values individual achievement.

I took the Myers-Briggs Personality test in the early 2000s and never really grasped all it was communicating about how I showed up and interacted with the world. I bought the book Strengths Finder in 2009 and did the assessments. Later, I took the DISC personality profile back in 2015, and again, it made little sense to me. Fast forward to 2023, I did the updated versions of Gallup Clifton Strengths and Myers-Briggs, and suddenly, the bells started going off. Everything started making sense to me because I was now ready to receive the lesson. I am not sure why it finally made sense, but life experiences had taught me enough, and I guess my eyes were finally opened to receive the lesson. I could now see myself in ways I had never conceived previously. Is it because I had deliberately slowed down long enough to observe myself and my interaction with the world around me? In 2023, I experienced a lot of intense emotions. I spent time examining and processing these feelings. I reflected on where these thoughts and emotions originated from. I also analyzed the behaviors and patterns that were controlling my life and leading to undesirable outcomes. I bravely confronted the less attractive aspects of myself and tried to show compassion to the parts of myself that I struggled to accept. I needed to improve for our children, marriage, families, community, and world.

> *Work harder on yourself than you do on your job.*
> —Jim Rohn

According to this philosophy, focusing on personal growth will attract success to you rather than the other way around. Instead of pursuing external markers of success like careers or societal definitions, focus on growing from within. When you invest in who you are, success will follow. Jobs may lay you off, pay you poorly, or mistreat you, but at the end of the day, you go home to yourself. If you're not growing, you're not improving your life. In this glamor and glitz culture, not all that glitter is gold. Don't get bamboozled. Come home to yourself, and know yourself, your weaknesses, and your strengths in order to survive and thrive in this country, or make no mistakes about it; you will be eaten alive. Someone or an entity who is sure of their self-interest will be waiting to use you, take your money, take your joy and peace, feed you garbage, and whatever they need to achieve their self-interest. Come home to yourself and discover the power and peace that was always there within you. The power is within you, not in this flashy, superficial, doing culture. You will not survive in this individualistic or collectivist culture if you are not home to yourself. Invest in yourself. Join a coaching program. Talent plus investment equals strength. Have you ever felt completely alive just by being aligned with your purpose? You wake up with energy and excitement, and you have new ideas every day. You feel connected to everything around you, attracting helpers and resources effortlessly. This is what it feels like to come home to yourself, to live with ease and flow. It's possible; I'm living that after years of searching and seeking understanding.

We know you are here on a mission. To achieve to the fullest and make others proud, how can you be your best self while pursuing said goals and decreasing hindrances and derailments? Sometimes, it is crucial to shed things that no longer serve us and grab hold of the new. How can God give you purpose if your hands are already full? Sometimes, too, it is important to know your roots, traditions, and heritage, or you may be lost in the new world. It is important to be wise in this culture of glitz and glam, fake body parts, and more falsehoods. How do you sort through the garbage to get to the gold and diamonds? This is where your community comes in as your eyes, ears and feelings when you cannot see clearly. So do not throw out the baby with the bath water. Find a way to use your superpower of being a TCP, belonging to both collectivist and individualistic cultures. Watch out for the sacrifice and savior mentality and immigrant survivor's guilt, and make space for mistakes, peace, joy, and whatever waters your soul.

> Discover what may be sabotaging your life. Take the saboteur assessment.
>
> positiveintelligence.com

Establishing credibility and generating trust is essential in this culture, so you must get comfortable with tooting your own horn and self-promotion. Be mindful of the modest mindset. It is certainly okay to share your accomplishments publicly, as this is how the professional world operates, but also watch out for that battle that takes place from the collectivist culture that tells you that self-promotion is bragging and boasting. Essentially, be intentional in building character and growing yourself over chasing the fleeting goal of success.

I recently watched the Disney children's movie "Moana" for the second time and was captivated. I was struck by the symbolism of Te Fiti discovering her true self as Moana restores her heart. The scene of Te Fiti losing her heart and turning into a monster, only to be restored when Moana returns it to her, was truly powerful.

As Moana restores Te Fiti's heart, a profound transformation sweeps through her like the first rays of dawn banishing the shadows of night. The once darkened and desolate land begins to blossom, mirroring her own renewal. She feels an overwhelming sense of peace and wholeness as if reuniting with a long-lost part of herself. The anger and pain that had consumed her as Te Kā dissipated, replaced by a deep serenity and a return to her true nature—life-giving and nurturing. In this moment of restoration, Te Fiti reconnects with her core essence, understanding that her power lies not in vengeance but in creation and love. Her journey back to herself symbolizes the power of forgiveness and the enduring strength of her spirit, embracing her role as the guardian of life once more.

As a first-generation immigrant, a child of immigrants, or a third-culture person, reclaiming one's sense of identity feels like a profound transformation, much like Te Fiti's journey of restoration. Navigating the complexities of multiple cultures, there comes a moment when we reconnect with our essence, embracing the unique blend of traditions, values, and experiences that shape who we are. The confusion and displacement that once clouded our sense of self begins to dissipate, replaced by a deep understanding and acceptance of our multifaceted identity. This journey back to ourselves symbolizes the power of resilience and the enduring strength of our spirit, celebrating the richness of our heritage while forging our path. In this moment of self-realization, we understand that our true power lies not in choosing one culture over another but in harmoniously blending them, creating a life that honors all parts of our story.

Becoming isn't about arriving somewhere or achieving a certain aim. I see it instead as forward motion, a means of evolving, a way to reach continuously toward a better self.

—Former First Lady, Michelle Obama

Embrace Who You Are Becoming Embrace Your Superpower

Many leave collectivist cultures in search of success and their individual selves but find that they lose themselves in the assimilation process. As shown throughout my story, the return was essential in Coming Home to Ourselves so that we could authentically stand in who we are. It is possible to acquire amazing success in the U.S. by surrendering to our life's calling/passion underpinned by a healthy knowledge of our cultural heritage and roots in who we are to achieve an integrated/balanced immigrant experience. It's not perfect, but I'm getting there. My immigrant experience brought me home to myself, and many are in the throes of it.

Who are you becoming? Are you happy with the life you are creating while building the life of your dreams in the land that flows with milk and honey? Are you still chasing the proverbial having it all? It is possible to have an integration of personal success with collective impact. Our coaching program calls it The Balanced-Integrated Immigrant Life. Have you acknowledged that you have changed? You are an integrated hybrid, a third-culture person - TCP of your birth and adopted country. Can you show up as your authentic [immigrant] self in your daily life and with the people who matter the most to you? The way to authenticity is honesty in a safe space. The space where what we want and do not want is respected, heard, and validated.

Authenticity frees you to be yourself and accept your flaws and all parts of yourself and leads to you being able to offer that same grace to others. It starts with you coming home to yourself. World peace begins with each of us finding peace within and expressing it to others. Compassion and grace for yourself as you walk through the immigrant experience as a third-culture bridge person create connection. According to Angelina Jolie, "Be yourself. Whether the world can handle it or not, it's not your problem." Is it possible as a first-generation immigrant to have the space to build the life you want? What will it cost to choose you and come home to yourself?

Are you familiar with the term 'Tall Poppy'? It is a cultural term used in collectivist and egalitarian societies to refer to people who stand out for their high abilities, enviable qualities, and visible success. In such societies, rising above the rest of the pack is considered antisocial and countercultural. This is known as the crab in a barrel effect in the United States.[7]

As a first-generation high achiever, have you experienced this? What impact has it had on your life and confidence? Despite putting in the work, studying hard, and sacrificing self-gratification underpinned by delayed gratification, those close to you may see you as a tall poppy. They call you a high achiever, even though they had the same, if not more, opportunities and squandered them or made different choices.

Remember, standing tall is something to be proud of, and you should not let anyone's negative views or opinions bring you down. Keep striving for success and continue to be a positive influence on those around you. We are here to support you in creating space for you to live the life you have worked so hard to realize. It can be isolating to be a tall poppy. The larger group may use shame or guilt to control you and get you to continue the roles that serve them but no longer serve you—perhaps never served you. Embrace who you are becoming. Embrace your superpower as a TCP. You can have a balanced immigrant life, expressing your individual success while having a community impact on your terms and timing.

There is a world where you do not have to operate solely from a place of duty or responsibility to others. You have done your part. There is space for your purpose and desires that pull you out of bed with motivation, energy, and clarity. In fact, you show up as a healthier version of yourself for all involved. A balanced, integrated immigrant life can work out for the highest good for all concerned. You do not have to sacrifice everything for the good of the collective.

Picture yourself climbing a mountain. The higher you go, the thinner the air gets. It becomes challenging traveling with weight or extra clothing. You will have to decide what to shed to get to higher ground. This was the vision that engulfed me on

---

7 Crabs in a barrel effect: Whenever someone gets ahead, others from their community try to pull them right back down again. This is similar to when a crab tries to climb out of a barrel; the others instinctively pull him back.

VISIT THE SCHOOL OF GREATNESS PODCAST AT: HTTPS://LEWISHOWES.COM/SOGPODCAST/

When you are pretending to be someone else, God cannot bless you. When I started walking in my freedom, [everyone] they disappeared. Everybody's not ready to walk in their freedom. Being close to you when you're in yours is disturbing their spirit. Could it be that you are depressed because you are out of alignment with who you are meant to be? Because I wasn't living my truth for long. I have created this Tabitha who would win. I was suffocating through me so I could be free. I learned how to mask my accent. When I worked in a call center, people would call and say, "Are you Black? I don't want to speak to somebody Black." Be neutral. No one should know where you're from.

My name, Tabitha, used to get me jobs because people thought I was White. It was conforming to survive. My ancestors had to do it to survive, and it was passed down. I am enough as myself. The thing I used to cover up about myself is what people like most about me now. Somebody sold me a lie, and I bought it, but I returned it and got all my money back. I'm from South Carolina. You know what you're dealing with, i.e., if someone likes you or not. Out here in LA, people be wearing masks. You'll think they like you when they actually don't. Showing up exactly who you are. Walking in your truth will allow the things that are for you to come. People who are blessed being someone they are not are miserable. They feel like they're not enough. You have everything but you feel unfulfilled, empty, no peace. They're always chasing something else. Freedom and being true to who you are is the best gift you can give yourself. Your truth is in your silence when no one else is around. The things you knew before you were taught that you weren't enough and before you believed it. We're born knowing what we're supposed to do, but we're influenced by our parents, friends, etc. Sometimes unintentionally.

my birthday in 2021, exactly six months after Mom passed. I had carried such a weight of responsibility and duty that often, I did not know how to slow down or stop the 'doing.' As I took a few days away to the Blue Ridge Mountains of Georgia, everything came rushing in. I had worked hard to be a good daughter. I studied, worked, and did my best to avoid anything that would embarrass my family, BUT it was not enough. All this pursuit of success took me away from my mom and others dear to me. I would only see them a few times per year. What is the point of chasing success if it means missing precious time with your loved ones? I cried, I prayed, and I yearned for another day with Mom. I had to find solace in the fact that I did the best I knew at the time. The name of the cabin was 'Higher Ground,' and as I circled the property early on my birthday, face washed in tears, I realized I needed to come home to myself. I was feeling empty from all the achieving. The downloads of all the things I needed to shed to get to higher ground all came rushing in: unforgiveness, lack of unhealthy and loose boundaries, the chase of achievements, unhealthy relationships, unhealthy choices, operating solely from a place of duty and responsibility, sacrificing myself, silencing my inner voice, giving away my energy, and the list goes on. I needed to find my joy, peace, and aliveness again. I believe that is where I made the decision to do a life audit of people, things, and activities present in my life, which sucked my energy and that did not feed my soul.

I would no longer take the next higher-paying job just because someone depended on me. There has to be a place to fuel my tank with what my soul hungered for while serving the community. I am so glad I did. I listened. I watered my garden. I said no and made space for me and my life to be a priority. Today, I am a healthy, wiser person for it. What will you shed? What do you need to shed to step into your superpowered, high-achieving immigrant self?

The U.S. is the place where we come to forget who we are, but you do not have to forget or lose yourself here. As an immigrant, you can intentionally create the balanced, integrated life you desire and deserve. You can choose to live today like no one else so that tomorrow, you can live like no one else. What parts of you have you lost? What are you holding on to from the former culture that no longer serves you and weighs you down? Will you choose to get to higher ground for the sake of the fullest expression of who God meant you to be? We can travel lighter, wiser, more joyful, and on purpose. As a hybrid—TCP of the collectivist and individualistic culture, your superpower is maximizing the best of both worlds.

Come home to yourself and use it to your advantage.

A strengths-based, culturally competent coaching program can ignite your superpower and give you the support you deserve to build the life you desire—the fullest, most expansive version of the life the creator and source of all life brought you here to express.

Come home with us today.

World peace depends on it.

You can find joy in the United States despite the troubling issues of suicide, violence, racial tension, and other challenges often faced by developed nations. Amid these difficulties, the country's remarkable achievements continue to inspire hope for immigrants worldwide. The U.S. can be seen as a level playing field for success, provided that barriers like racism, prejudice, and other 'isms' do not hinder progress. Learning to navigate these complexities is crucial, especially when you know how to 'come home to yourself.'

Embrace that journey.

Come home.

As I reflect on the journey of bringing this book to life, I am filled with gratitude for the incredible individuals who have supported and inspired me along the way. Each of you has played a vital role in shaping this project, and I want to take a moment to acknowledge your contributions.

To my husband, Jimmy: You have witnessed my deepest struggles and the most broken parts of my journey, yet your unwavering strength has breathed life back into me time and again. You steady me and bring balance to my life in ways I never knew I needed. God brought you into my life to help me nurture my own garden when it felt dry, depleted, and burned out. Thank you for being my man of steel while leading with a gentle, steady hand. Your love and support have made all the difference, and I am eternally grateful.

To my editor, Lena Joy Rose: You were the mentor, guide, and steady hand I needed to move this passion project forward. Thank you for your authentic insights that kept me focused and motivated, providing the perspective I needed to see this through.

To my podcast guests: You helped me start it all! When I stepped out in October 2020 with the initial idea, your willingness to share your immigrant journeys made it easy to launch. I am forever grateful for your vulnerability and strength; your stories inspired me and enriched this work in immeasurable ways. Thank you for being an integral part of this journey.

To Dr. Carol Edwards: Thank you for graciously reading this manuscript during our trip to Jamaica. Your thoughtful feedback was invaluable and deeply appreciated.

To Edward and Rochelle Wright: Your family has been with me since the beginning of my immigrant journey, having met in Kmart all those years ago. Your unwavering support, wise advice, and genuine care for my well-being have been a constant source of strength. I am truly grateful for your presence in my life.

To my beloved family:

(i) Grandmas Louise and Daisy; Grandpas Stephen and Albert: Your outstretched hands and countless sacrifices have shaped our family legacy for generations. Thank you for all that you have given us.

(ii) Mom (Merdit): We miss your calming presence every day. I wish I had captured more of your incredible journey and immigrant story, but I feel your guidance with us always.

(iii) Dad (Linton): Thank you for your steadfast leadership and strength. I deeply appreciate the sacrifices you've made for our family.

(iv) Extended Family: I am grateful for both the joyful moments and the challenges we've faced together. Each of you has played a vital role in shaping who I am today.

(v) My friends -- my chosen family: Your support brings me balance, purpose, and the motivation to make this world a better place. Thank you for being in my life.

Simone Johnson Smith is a passionate life coach, speaker, and author dedicated to amplifying the voices of immigrants. She hosts the acclaimed podcast *The Immigrant Experience in America*, which features over 160 episodes and has been nominated as one of the top 20 American culture podcasts, reaching listeners in more than 50 countries.

Since migrating from Jamaica to the U.S., Simone's personal journey has deeply informed her understanding of the daily challenges immigrants face. Drawing from her experiences as a former U.S. Diplomat and federal employee, she recognized a significant gap in awareness regarding the valuable contributions immigrants make to American society. In her book, *Decoding America & Coming Home to Yourself: The Immigrant Experience*, she offers a practical roadmap to help immigrants navigate their new environment and thrive in their adopted country.

Simone believes that effectively bridging collectivist and individualistic cultures requires profound self-exploration, coaching, and continuous learning.

Outside of her professional endeavors, she enjoys music and nature, staying active, and exploring diverse cultures both domestically and internationally. Simone currently lives in the southeastern United States with her husband and daughter.

UNLOCK YOUR GLOBAL POTENTIAL WITH THE THRIVING ABROAD COACHING PROGRAM

Are you an expat, international professional, or someone about to embark on a journey abroad? Navigating life in a new country can be both exhilarating and challenging. The **Thriving Abroad Coaching** program is here to ensure you not only survive but thrive in your new environment!

WHAT WE OFFER:

 **Personalized Coaching:** Tailored sessions designed to address your unique challenges and goals while living abroad.

 **Cultural Adaptation:** Gain insights into local customs, communication styles, and social norms to help you integrate smoothly and confidently.

 **Career Success:** Strategies to excel in your career, whether you're adjusting to a new job market, building professional networks, or seeking career growth abroad.

 **Resilience Building:** Develop the mental and emotional resilience needed to handle the ups and downs of expatriate life.

 **Community and Support:** Join a network of like-minded individuals on similar journeys, offering mutual support and shared experiences.

WHY CHOOSE THRIVING ABROAD COACHING?

Our experienced coaches have lived and worked abroad, and they understand the complexities of international transitions. We're committed to helping you find balance, achieve your goals, and create a fulfilling life abroad.

READY TO THRIVE?

Don't just live abroad—thrive abroad! Join our program today and start your journey towards a successful and fulfilling life in your new home. Jumpstart your transformation with a FREE coaching session at: **https://thebridgeconcepts.org/thriving-abroad-coaching/**

REFERENCES

1. Chopra, D. (1994). The Seven Spiritual Laws of Success: A Practical Guide to the Fulfillment of Your Dreams. Amber-Allen Publishing.

2. Coughlin, P., & Degler, J. D. (2010). No more Christian nice girl: When just being nice—instead of good—hurts you, your family, and your friends. Revell

3. Denslow, L. (2005). Working with Americans: How to Communicate, Collaborate, and Work Effectively with Americans. Intercultural Press.

4. Dispenza, J. (2012). Breaking the Habit of Being Yourself: How to Lose Your Mind and Create a New One. Hay House.

5. Dufu, T. (2017). Drop the Ball: Achieving More by Doing Less. Harper Business.

6. Gordon, J. (2007). The Energy Bus: 10 Rules to Fuel Your Life, Work, and Team with Positive Energy. Wiley.

7. Jones-DeWeever, A. (2021). How Exceptional Black Women Lead. Amistad.

8. Moran, B. P. (2013). The 12 Week Year: Get More Done in 12 Weeks than Others Do in 12 Months. Wiley.

9. Murphy, J. (2005). The Power of Your Subconscious Mind. Atria Books.

10. Tawwab, N. G. (2021). Set Boundaries, Find Peace: A Guide to Reclaiming Yourself. TarcherPerigee.

11. Tolle, E. (1997). The Power of Now: A Guide to Spiritual Enlightenment. New World Library.

12. Tolle, E. (2005). A New Earth: Awakening to Your Life's Purpose. Penguin Group.

i. U.S. Conference of Catholic Bishops. How the Civil Rights Movement Influenced U.S. Immigration Policy. Retrieved from: https://www.usccb.org/committees/african-american-affairs/how-civil-rightsmovement-influenced-us-immigration-policy.

ii. American Enterprise Institute. Affirmative Action Helps Black Immigrants but Not Black Americans. Retrieved from: https://www.aei.org/op-eds/affirmative-action-helps-black-immigrants-butnot-black-americans/

iii. Top Colleges Take More Blacks, but Which Ones? The New York Times. Retrieved from: https://www.nytimes.com/2004/06/24/us/top-colleges-take-more-blacks-butwhich-ones.html

iv. *Forbes.* Immigrants Make Economies More Dynamic, Increase Employment Growth. Retrieved from: https://www.forbes.com/sites/stuartanderson/2023/02/23/immigrants-makeeconomies-more-dynamic-increase-employment-growth/?sh=7091d764427c

v. *Forbes.* Highly Inventive Immigrants Also Make Natives More Innovative. Retrieved from: https://www.forbes.com/sites/stuartanderson/2023/01/12/highly-inventiveimmigrants-also-make-natives-more-innovative/?sh=71f5775d324b.

vi. American Immigration Council. New Report Reveals Immigrant Roots of Fortune 500 Companies. Retrieved from: https://www.americanimmigrationcouncil.org/news/new-report-revealsimmigrant-roots-fortune-500-companies.

vii. NFAP Policy Brief: AI and Immigrants. NFAP.

viii. Kauffman Compilation: Immigration and Entrepreneurship (PDF). Retrieved from: kauffman_compilation_immigration_entrepreneurship.pdf

ix. The White House. Ten Ways Immigrants Help Build and Strengthen Our Economy. Retrieved from: https://www.whitehouse.gov

x. *Forbes.* Evidence Mounts That Reducing Immigration Harms America's Economy. Retrieved from: https://www.forbes.com/sites/stuartanderson/2021/04/01/evidence-mountsthat-reducing-immigration-harms-americas-economy/?sh=6c39dce9202c.

xi. Pardee Center for the Study of the Longer-Range Future. The Anti-Immigrant Movement in the United States. Retrieved from: https://sites.bu.edu/pardeeatlas/advancing-human-progress-initiative/back2school/the-antiimmigrant-movement-in-the-united-states/

xiii. Harvard University. Historical Context of Immigration Policy and Sentiment Today: Q&A with Moshik Temkin. Retrieved from: https://ash.harvard.edu/news/historical-context-immigration-policy-andsentiment-today-qa-moshik-temki

xiv. Harvard University. Early 20th Century Historical Context. Retrieved from: https://ash.harvard.edu/news/historical-contextimmigration-policy-and-sentiment-today-qa-moshik-temkin

xvi. University of California Press. America's Long History of Anti-immigrant Sentiment and the Policing of Movement. Retrieved from: https://www.ucpress.edu/blog/43467/americas-long-history-ofanti-immigrant-sentiment-and-policing-of-movement/

xvii. Global Citizen. The 7 Biggest Challenges Facing Refugees and Immigrants. Retrieved from: https://www.globalcitizen.org/en/content/the-7-biggest-challenges-facingrefugees-and-immig/

xviii. Caesar, James W. AMERICAN EXCEPTIONALISM: IS IT REAL, IS IT GOOD? Origins and Character of American Exceptionalism. Retrieved from: https://time.com/wp-content/uploads/2015/02/ceaser.pdf

xix. *Encyclopaedia Britannica.* American Exceptionalism. Retrieved from: https://www.britannica.com/topic/American-exceptionalism

xx. Ethics & International Affairs. What is American Exceptionalism? Retrieved from: https://www.ethicsandinternationalaffairs.org/online-exclusives/what-isamerican-exceptionalism

xxi. *Psychology Today.* What is Code-Switching? Retrieved from: https://www.psychologytoday.com/us/blog/achieving-health-equity/202012/what-is-code-switching

xxii. G2. What is Cross-Cultural Communication? Retrieved from: https://www.g2.com/articles/what-is-cross-cultural-communication

xxiii. *Southern Living.* Bless My Heart: Self-Directed Sympathy. Retrieved from: https://www.southernliving.com/culture/bless-your-heart-response

xxiv. Cleveland Clinic. What Are Microaggressions and Examples? Retrieved from: https://health.clevelandclinic.org/what-are-microaggressions-and-examples; *Psychology Today.* Microaggression. Retrieved from: https://www.psychologytoday.com/us/basics/microaggression; NPR. Microaggressions Are a Big Deal: How to Talk Them Out and When to Walk Away. Retrieved from: https://www.npr.org/2020/06/08/872371063/microaggressions-are-a-big-deal-how-to-talk-them-out-and-when-to-walk-away

xxv. Books: *Set Boundaries Find Peace, Co-dependent No More and Boundaries.*

xxvi. *Forbes.* The Struggles of a First-Generation Immigrant. Retrieved from: https://www.forbes.com/sites/forbeseq/2021/12/20/the-strugglesof-a-first-generation-immigrant/?sh=1f5efa1e1953 and Why is There a Higher Rate of Imposter Syndrome Among BIPOC? Retrieved from: https://projects.iq.harvard.edu/files/isl/files/why_is_there_a_higher_rate_of_imposter_syndrome_among_bipoc_1.pdf

xxvii. NPR. Weathering: Arline Geronimus, Poverty, Racism, Stress, Health. Retrieved from: https://www.npr.org/sections/health-shots/2023/03/28/1166404485/weatheringarline-geronimus-poverty-racism-stress-health; Medical News Today. Weathering: What Are the Health Effects of Stress and Discrimination? Retrieved from: https://www.medicalnewstoday.com/articles/weathering-what-are-the-health-effects-of-stress-and-discrimination

xxviii. https://www.forbes.com/sites/forbeseq/2021/12/20/the-struggles-of-a-firstgeneration-immigrant/?sh=1f5efa1e1953[12]

xxix. See also chronic stress. [first described in the context of psychology around 1940 by Hungarian-born Canadian endocrinologist Hans Selye (1907–1982)] (https://dictionary.apa.org/stress)

xxx. Stress and its manifestations: (https://www.psychologytoday.com/us/basics/stress)

xxxi. World Health Organization on stress: (https://www.who.int/news-room/questions-and-answers/item/stress)

xxxii. Burnout: (https://dictionary.apa.org/burnout).

xxxiii. Symptoms of burnout: (https://www.ncbi.nlm.nih.gov/books/NBK279286/)

xxxiv. Myers Briggs, DISC, Clifton Strengths, Saboteur Assessment—share your results and discuss how important it is to know yourself when you come home to yourself. https://www.linkedin.com/posts/eric-partaker-5560b92_7-ted-talksin-7-days-to-live-your-happiest-activity-7133801002159226880-4KnP?utm_source=share&utm_medium=member_desktop

xxxv. Micro, Meso and Exosystems: https://doi.org/10.1111/ijsw.12595

xxxvi. On burnout in high achieving women: https://www.betsyjordyn.com/blog/why-high-achieving-women-burn-out

xxxvii. On burnout in high achieving women: https://www.sparkcounseling.com/blog/navigatingburnoutwithmulticultural counseling https://ballardbrief.byu.edu/issue-briefs/barriers-to-career-advancementamong-skilled-immigrants-in-the-us https://www.apa.org/monitor/2021/10/cover-parental-burnout https://www.researchgate.net/publication/297660350_Social_Determinants_of_Immigrant_Women's_Mental_Health

xxxviii. Coping strategies to counter burnout: https://www.calmwaterspllc.com/burnout out